Boyz Burlesque

By Strang

Glover Lane Press
Publishers Since January 2000
www.gloverlanepress.webs.com

Boyz Burlesque Conceived & Performed by Strang

Copyright 2014 by Strang for Strangu Prods.

Cover Design by Azaan Kamau & Strang

ISBN-13: 978-0615968520
ISBN-10: 061596852X

The Mission of Glover Lane Press is to Uplift, Empower, Elevate the Masses and
Provide American Jobs. Every book published by Glover Lane Press and its many
imprints, is printed and manufactured in the United States of America, ensuring and
maintaining American employment.

Accolades

"Each poem has a special story of its own! These poems will touch everybody in its own way! Excited about the finished product"! -Jerimy Gilley

"Excellent read! Passionate and colorful poetry that everyone can relate to"!-Jackie Nelson

"Organic Poetry from a raw organic soul"!-Trey L. Harris

"Anari's Poetry is a chilling symphony of colors and textures. At times unforgiving yet, beautifully floral and romantic"!-Utopia Healing

~Curtain Calls~

To my family ~ "My cup runneth over"!

To my friends ~ Thank you for loving, encouraging & for just simply putting up with me...

"See you all backstage"!

Azaan & Glp...Thank you for believing in me & my act.

And, (Of Course) For having such a warm & embraceable spirit.

I am eternally humbled... "Now let's take my show to the world" (lolll) :-)

To the reader...

Much appreciation & gratitude I extend to you.

May this book compel & unveil your "boyz burlesque"!

~Honorary dedication~

This book is dedicated to my brother "Kevin d. Davis"

(The Professor)

"So the words you could not say, I'll sing them for you"!

"To the life you never had the chance to live,

I vow to live it for you"!

R.I.P. May your wings forever outrun the sky

I love you, your brother...a!

Che' (G. bleu)

I think of you & miss you immensely (you will never know how much)

It is because of you that my "boyz burlesque" abounds.

So what else is there left to say but...

sit back, relax and Njoy the show...

"You shameless craven, you"! (hahahahaa)

Love, your friend...A. Strang!

Mrs. S. Bookspan

I hope & pray this book makes you proud.

You've taught me so much about the beauty of poetry

and the most effective lesson learned is...

"Sometimes less is best"!

I will forever carry this philosophy, & the memory of you.

Love, your pupil...a!

Now on with the show......

~The Playbill~

If ...."I've come to learn... "NOT TO TEACH"!!!

Gitn2itbytch.."Today's Trade, Tomorrow's Competition"!

Hush Money............................"The Rich transitions to a Bitch, The Poor...A Whore"!

Daddy's LunchBoxxx............There's a party in my pants..."AND EVERY-1's CUMMIN"!

Adolescent Delicatessen................"For the right price, you too can feed on my pride"!

Death certificate/Blak Majik............................You tried to love me, you gave it a twist. "But it ended in a drip of blood... From a Lip to a Fist"!

Corey 16.........................Another innocence dead..."And now let's all bow our heads"!

Subway Red.. "Love is a 1-way street, if I'm lost & stranded"!

Ragtime............................I've gotta stop wishing you death, if I intend on staying alive. I've gotta sage my heart & stop all this drinking at 5... (Am that is, lol)

And he runs..When the loving ran out, "He ran out with it"!
And I run...Got on my best running shoes, "Here I go.....

Marshmallow Boy...."A Little Brains, a little talent, "With an emphasis on the Latter"!

Gypsy mama blaque.................."You need dreams to live, & the Truth to Die in Peace"!

World's Fair/Carnivale...................................."Pay to get in....."PRAY TO GET OUT"!

He had it comin......................................."Tell me you wouldn't have done the same"!

Ham ....The silly in me, in all his idiosyncrasies!

Kid (dedicated to Sir Chaplin)....................."Streets of Berlin...........Will you miss me, was I ever really here"?

Torchsong.."Don't let's ask for the moon...We have the stars"!

Black winter..."Believe in Love "Just not it's Warranty"!

Rasputin.."There never was a love like mine for you, & there never will be"!

Nutcracker (dedicated to Ms. Stanwyck)..................."I committed murder to get you"!

Seasick.."You may be the party... "BUT I AM THE FUN"!

Apathy..."I'm too old of a cat To be Fucked by a Pussy"!

My Dik iz the Lik...................."To all of the Schlongs in the world, "Let us unite"! (ha)

Valerie.........................Rejection can be a damaging effect..."Or a maturing prospect"!

Misconceptions ....Sometimes it hurts like hell just trying to be a man. "Do You Agree"?

Men-Oh-Pause/Diet..........................."I'm starving...but not for what you're feeding"!

My Ashes (dedicated to Che' & "The Professor")......................."Where are you going, Where is everybody going?

Cinderfella/ 3rd Son........"Just cause we're family, doesn't mean we must be friends"!

Ni__hwyte..."Any man running from who he is within, is life's worst sin"!

Whyteni__h ...."How you gon know where I'm at, if you ain't been where I've been"? Understand where I'm coming from?

Drug.."C'mon baby, c'mon daddy, I need my fix"!

Medicine.."Damn, whatta hangover"!

Hoebath..Loving you is like... "Whew"!!!

Friendzzzz..Good or bad, you've gotta have em!

I can't F_ck witchu.......................You're forbidden candy, & yet I just can't resist you...
("Damn You")!

Mr. Ms.-tress..."I don't wanna wear your name...
I just wanna make you feel some thangs"!
The tears of St. John..."Let my heart be still,
and listen to one song of love"! "Let me feel the thrill, of a quiet we know nothing of"!

A night of Porn... Donation... Do you give or do you take"?

American life/American dream enter-view
pt.1...Success can be bittersweet.
"But don't be deceived, by the measures one will go to achieve it"!

Caveman pt.2..To the 1 I love: You know who you are.
I don't, but you do. When we meet, this will all at last make sense.
Until then, let's just kick back sip, snack & Njoy the suspense"!

Church home... "This is just between you & me"!

Boyz burlesque................................."If you want to understand me...Read My Poetry"!

No, your girl can't watch.."Father Christian man, is it true...
"That all the boys wanna cum on you"? (Cool, but not if she's with you)

~The Invitation~

"Step right up, step right up ladies & gentlemen"!
"Incidentally... Would you like me to seduce you"?

I am reserved, I am loud
I am humble, yet fiercely proud
I am flawless, lawless, I delight, I inspire
I am water, ether, earth & fire
I am the prince of darkness, his phantom's dance
I am my mistress' eyes never giving way to time & chance
I am prodigal, a partisan with planets aligned
I am the heart of Adam, the breath of his sheep
I am fantasies & dreams even when I'm not asleep
I am pandemonium, controversial
A Shakespearean renaissance-I am universal
I am geisha to her king
I am Lazarus' heart- "Stab its Sting"-(Then watch me sing)
I am surrender without sacrifice
I am Shangri-la, with or without ice ("Mmm, hmm")
I am my virgin's smile, an addictive ingenue'
I am he-she-me & u
I am Neptune's veil, a Summoner's tale,
A harlequin's marionette
I am Stravinsky's symphony adorned in Cavafy's silhouette
I am sinner & yet a saint
"I am"... (Even when others say I ain't)
I am beauty & the beast
I am raven's wine, before & after the feast
I am the Wizard & the Witch, the Pimp & his Bitch
I am music, magic, life, death, poetry, art & sex
I am "DRAMA"...one after the next
I am passion's penetration... "Care for a demonstration"?

I am myth, mayhem, mystery-A pauper's peasant
I am "Phenomenal Man"... past, future & present
I am Mercury's moon, Poseidon's quasar
I am my warrior's wound, the outlaw laying down his scars
I am tears & laughter-An "Orphan's Opus"!
I am truth, I am lies
I am the serpent's kiss, to either desire or despise
I am boy, I am girl
I am the blood of his divine... "Naked to the World"!
I am peace, pride, infinite wisdom,
An epiphany just because
I am all, I am one, for I am... "Love"!

Now...
Close the doors, settle in
"Lights down, Curtains up-"Shh", hush up
For the show's about to begin...

If

If you were a tongue, I'd be your saliva
If you were a horse, I'd be your Godiva
If you were peace, I'd be war
If you were a pimp, I'd be your whore
If you were a scar, I'd be the wound
If you were a star, I'd be your moon
If you were sweat, I'd be its funk
If you're pussy, then I'm the funk

You're beautiful, salaciously tempting
How could I ever refuse you
Damn, if you were mine I'd never want to bruise you or lose you
You intensify me, from articuation to physical affectation
You drive the inner-me straight into the borders of lust & matrimony
Oh if,

If...
If you were a sailor, I'd be the sea
If you were Sir Olivier, then I'm Lady Leigh
If you were crack, I'm the pipe
If you were the internet, I'm your website
If you were a stripper, I'm the pole
If you're Leopold, I'm your Loeb
If you were photography, I'd be your expose'
If you were a crime, I'm the DNA

I find I'm walking on a thin-line
Excitedly, even at the mention of your name
I relinquish all thoughts enchained to resistance & shame
I fold, as you take hold of my soul with every smile you centerfold
Seducing me & my inner-kitty beyond taboos & vulnerability
Desiring, if nothing less, just a kiss to pamper an unspoken bliss
Oh if,

My God if...
If you were pornography, I'd be your every fantasy
If you were sins, I'm your confession on worn torn knee
If you're the party, I'm the fun
If you're in love, then let me be the only one
If you were a song, I'm the melody
If you're an addiction, I'm your sobriety
If you're heaven, I'm Satan's spawn
If it is "YOU", then you're the obsession this poem is based upon
If you're champagne, I'm the glass
If you're the first, then I'm forever the last

Nature of the beast, an inevitable fate
And since "IF" is a crooked letter that will never be straight
Keep steppin kid... You've come 10 years too late-Oh if,
Damn, If only if???

gitn2itbytch (aha)

Yo...
Yo dick might be bigger
But I still can fuck yo niggah-(aha) "gitn2itbytch"
You got a baby face, 28inch waist
So why is yo niggah all up in my face-(aha) "gitn2itbytch"
You got D.S.L. (dick sucking lips) skillz,
Denali wheels, side gig hustling meth rocks & E-pills
Still, yo niggah's robbin from you to come pay my billz
(aha) "gitn2itbytch"

Tell me, is it really that cool, being that much a fool
It's obvious you're stuck on stupid, believing that cupid
Would sweat a dude that ain't even checkin 4 u
Mercy me, the gay youth, to tell you the truth-Some of y'all today...
Dickhounded, Dumbfounded, Disillusioned & Desperate
Convincing yourself that the only way I can pull some young dick
Is if I'm paying for it
Cause everybody knows that once you cross the threshold to getting old
Who really wants to trick with a geriatric... "Your man does"!
And while he leaves you sittin fumin in the dark
I'll be the witch to flick on the switch to pitch... (aha) "gitn2itbytch"

Shit...
You got a stripper's body
You do Yoga, Pilates, Kabbalah, even karate
Still the rhythm in my rump, makes yo niggah pump & jump
(aha) "gitn2itbytch"
So what...
You got a bachelor's & master's degree, a Magna cum Lade
Still it's me he loves with an EET & G.E.D-(aha) "gitn2itbytch"
And who really gives a F_CK...
That you got the latest I-POD, I-PAD & I-Phone
Even got a pimped out penthouse flat to call your own
But that ain't where yo niggah's livin at, which in fact
Is why you always end up sleeping alone-(aha) "gitn2itbytch"

You know the latest dance
NE Yo, Rhianna, Beyonce even Lady GA Ga Jams
Rocking skater pants with matching vans, yet in all this circumstance
It's yo niggah that's dying to sop, what's copped in my pants
(aha) "gitn2itbytch"

Go on, call me a bitter convalescent queen
A pasty-wrinkly has-been old news 2 the scene
Who gets no sex in the sheets, no love in the clubs
And who only rages whenever he's surrounded by queenagers
Surely you jest, looka here & check your playbill...Ms. Drama Overkill
Don't trip, nor get it twisted
Cause even with all the Grey sprayed across my chinny-chin-chin,
The wrinkles crinkled throughout my skin,
the pudge fudged in my cellulite
None will prevent me from whooping your ass
Should you wanna test me tonite
So let's keep it cute... "Pretty, Aiight"!

Cause I know it racks your brain, ("Don't it")
Drives your juvenile wiles insane ("Oh agony, the pain")
Because you can't comprehend why any man
Who's taut & commercially hot would wanna fuck wit the likes of me
Maybe if you'd stop watching your weight, carbs, fat & sugar intake
Curb your shady-assed attitude, that's so prude, rude & fake
Adopt some couth & caliber
Something more organic, pragmatic & a little less Dramatic
Recognize I've paved the runways you now tread
So instead of hating you should be congratulating
One's, moralistic philosophy-Say, this is just my observation
But if you wish, then go ahead my lil chickadee
Proceed with all your cracks & reads
A rag, an ole assisted living fag, a witch
I'll be sure to use that same expletive on your man
while he's sucking my dick
Now like I said... "GITN2ITBYTCH"!!!

hush money

Oh Hell, here we go again
Oh well, another episode of a fag fairytale
Mr Peter, Peter, Pinga Eater
Mr. Mother Goose, Mr. Hump Me, Dump Me
Then altogether turn me loose
Hoebaths & Booty calls
Muthafuckas that wanna bump meth, coke, poppers
while sniffing my drawls
Masters, slaves, bears, cubs even corporate cohorts
Recognize this escort's too credible to be broke
Bastards won't catch me slippin
Cause if I'm flippin, his ass is dippin me some...Hush money

I want the clothes, cars, the European trips
The finest wines that Rhianna, Mariah & Madonna sips
Exotic jewels pooled in a Swiss bank-Sorry to be so frank
But listen up chummy, this time around,
If I'm gonna be your secret slut bunny
Then you better hop your ass down to the nearest bank
To yank me out some...Hush Money

No cash=No ass
Save your crass, what's in it for me-Is my only concern
I take stocks, shares, equity, platinum & gold
A hustler's time, is never 5 & dime
So my sex will never be underrated nor undersold
Fuck matrimony-I prefer alimony
And to the dude who wants me as his private honey
Then he's pouring all over me some...Hush money

Am I a hoe? No!
Am I 3rd rate or cheap? Not even in my sleep!!!
You tell me...
Why should I have nothing to show, glow or brag
But starvation's impregnation grinding my back
And wet panties in a brown paper bag

Time is a terrible fate-Skin thins & looks fade
Shit, I ain't no dummy
You wanna adopt me as your fuck-buddy
First you signing me over some...Hush money

So here's to all my 2nd hunnies
Or if you're a 3rd, 4th, 5th, Shit, even 6
Before you suck his dick-Make sure that trick
Deposits you some...Hush money

If you're a Go-Go boy, house boy or a mere boy toy
Don't be coy, unless you employ...Hush Money
If you're a street hick or a D.L. Thug, with a 10inch dick
Before he gets a lick, tell that trick to flick you some...Hush Money

Your ass is an asset, your kiss is a commodity
Take a lesson from a vixen veteran
I don't care if you're under aged, middle aged, coffin aged
Single, married or newly engaged
If I'm dropping my drawls, you'd better withdrawal me some...
Hush Money

It's only evident
That 2 hungry mouths can't feed each other
And in my house, ain't nothing going on but the rent
So in order for us to bump cocks-I'ma need the cheese & stocks
Locked up in my safe deposit box
Mr. Mistress or Mr. Concubine, in the meantime
Wine, dine & some.....Hush Money!

daddy's lunchboxxx

Whenever I'm famished or craving
Savagely, I go racing to...
My daddy's lunchboxxx
It's...
Hard as a nickel
Thick as a pickle
Sweet & Juicy
Like a Cherry Popsicle

It takes me through...
Dungeon rooms, neon corridors
Grunge grooms fucking their Leather whores
Submission to sadism, one's pornographic pleasure
A mouthwatering encounter...
The second u & I are together
Sexual smorgasbord, nymphomaniac's menu
The beast devours his feast
Now let us continue...

Whenever my mouth needs a feeding
There's only one morsel it's needing...
My daddy's lunchboxxx
It's...
Hot like Java
Thick like lava
Sweet & Juicy
Like Vodka Guava

It takes me down to...
Liquid haze, Crystal ice
69 ways to troff in a pig's paradise
Inch 4 inch, pound 4 pound
Chests of fur-You "GRRRRR, I'll PURRRR"!
Into the cave where the bear and his cub become one
You, my vulgar vulture
Attack bareback, to then chump on my "CUMDUMP"!

Raunchy recipes, appetizing images
Gagged & hogtied, spanked with rawhide
Scrimmages fetishes of the flesh, if nothing less

Whenever I just get the munchies
And my hunger pang swells, that's when I run like hell to...
My Daddy's lunchboxxx
It's...
Meaty like a steak
Hearty like the 1 I just ate
Sweet & juicy
Like his Man-Goo pooled all over my face
A tasty dependency
A nourishing delight
A scrumptious delicacy
That more than stirs, wets & soothes my appetite
Apples, bananas, raisins & crackers
I'm starving to slave
So tell me Daddy...Will you be my master?

adolescent delicatessen

Circuit club outlaws-Slurp crystal licorice hash
Silence, you gutter trash
Simply flash Twink zombies, then catalog virginal Abercrombies
Southern born delight-Parlay "D.L". porn snippets
Advertise website's overbite
Feature mayhem's matinee... At $3.50 a ticket

Hormonal rebellion, their immaculate filth glistens
Herald onto its craze, bathe in Pre-Cum mayonnaise, then listen...
To their flirtatious lesson-Adolescent Delicatessen
Suffer a surrogate hunger their desires examine
An indecent indiscretion-Entree...Vanity's complexion
Its infection goes stealing down
"Top-or-Bottom"-Fresh-N-Stock-"Yep", we got em"
Snort alongside punk pin-ups-Feast on the beast who's new in town
Prognosis: Either feast or famine!

Skater Skid Boys
Profile West Hollywood abs
Tutor their obedient noise
For it's the flesh "At Best"
That collectively lies on the slab
Toys 4 Tots
Double-Down generic Kamikaze shots
Pop-a-Pill-(Watch it fizz)-Queer overkill
Up for the challenge-Take the quiz
Then just before noon's break
We'll meet to compete to see
Whose lineage dies first at the stake

A chilling discern
When governing a Hoe-Harem's introversion
One "Booty-Bump" to cure young Billy's heartburn
Before getting slaughterec by a bear's thoroughfare
(Not to mention his ungodly perversions)

Gym, Drugs, Soy, Sandals,
Fem boys perched upon Hamburger Mary's mantle
Reality show Hoe's being pimped for pennies
Praise thee... Anorexic ally
Slum's silhouette-A drag on his Meth Cigarette
As his ribcage takes center stage
Mr. Self-righteous, Ms. Salvation
Bitch I got my education, so stop hatin on me
Simply because my degree's in street poverty
And you're pushin 50

Love-Lust propositions
Pubes musk, Knees scab
Lick around the pudge his grunge bellies
Front row at the Tomkat, or backseat in a DC cab
Fare: $48 Tab, for STD'S Clinical labs
Incoherent oppositions
Innocence raped then draped in an alley's stench
Christen momma's pigtail boy's trilogy
A familiar corpse-Never mind giving his eulogy
Forgiveness is waif, for his pride has long died
Even before his lips & ass-crack turned chafe

A masochistic inflection-Adolescent Delicatessen
Worship cravings that diffuse self-worth & self-esteem
Fuck the "American Life-American Dream"!
Let's all gorge off our heart's inflections
Fuck them with or without limp erections
Back-2-Front-I'm the "Cock Jock" that every man wants
Bareback artificial stunts-Pop culture vultures
Milking blood cries from a beauty queen
Finality: Me at age 19
Being buried beneath a rat's ravine!
("MMMMMmmmmm")

blaque majik (death certificate)

Chapter 1
Look at you
Comatose, horrifically bruised
Boy of 22, once again laid up in ICU
IV'S plugged in your veins
You're lucky to be subdued, half-alive
Prognosis: a bullet lodged in your brain
Tranquilized by love
Kept by wealth-Subdued in sex & yet paralyzed with fear
A despicable defect, yet you choose to protect
The S.O.B. who's brought you here
A culmination of control & manipulation
You sass or debate and it's another case of strangulation
He slaps your face, you just shake off the sting
Then sink in drink after drink hoping to alleviate all of your pain
Cause brother can't live on one wing
What's it gonna take in order for you to break free
Domestic abuse victim, you're just another statistic living amongst them
An anthology of apologies aligned with fuck-sympathies
Or the pastor officiating your eulogy
Love, Thy will be done: A Perilous predicament
When it's the perpetrator who signs your death certificate

Chapter 2
And in comes a flurry of "Bitch-Hoes, Bitch Go's"!
He so lovingly tosses at you
Subservient, Self-gratification
He spits & spews his demands, & expects you
To meet each one on command
Sleepless nights, date-rape fights
The quality of mercy does not apply
Should you return to the scene of the crime
With another broken nose & a purple black eye

Well what's the point in calling the cops
They drag him out barefoot in cuffs
As your dumb ass is running from behind yelling
"Don't hurt him, I still love him"!
While posting bonds to bail his worthless ass out
Absurd to the naked eye, pathetic to the unfortunate
That such dysfunction can serve as a desperate bluff
Fore it's obvious to everyone that he hasn't kicked your ass enough

The blood floods, expletives exchanges
Cry in silence, talcum the pain
Spousal violence implores, yet forgiveness is the plot
Since he's convinced you that you're nothing without him
And he's all you've got

"Oh Father, as you kneel to pray for those of Monstrous eyes
My how they connive, yet constantly apologize
Love, thy will be done: One's daunting fate
Should the captive of your heart, be the one to chart your
Death Certificate

Chapter 3
Blaque Majik's bliss
Coin the phrase, you'll find tragedy on every page
Misery's twist
Pride's handicapped, your esteem is now under attack
Down for the count in just the 2nd round
And with just a kiss
His malice knows no couth or bounds
He belittles you, then cuddles you
Whenever your family & friends come around
Confusion circulates round the perimeters of love & hate
He consoles, controls
Smothers you with sex-shifts & guilt-gifts
You delight, pretend, give in
And with such sin...Peace is restored, the abuse ends

You even smile for a while
Hmph...Never underestimate the power of desperation & denial
Silent sorrow, stay tuned for the abuse he'll induce by tomorrow
Only now the Gods have spoken
As the angels has chosen to collect your sweet spirit
With an assurance that his fists will never again come near it
The tears he weeps will serve as a punishable edict
Your immortality will mark his grave, enslave until ultimately defeated
His hell will be a terminal welt, and only then will he begin to suffer
All the cheating & beatings you've felt
Assess all the damage, then contend...
Love Thy will be done: Finality, "Funeral for a Friend"
The End!!!

corey 16

I read somewhere in the news today
A boy named Corey 16 committed suicide just yesterday
A small farming town boy
There he was, found hung by the neck
Dangling from an oak tree inches away from his grandparent's barn
Swinging lifeless & naked
Stripped of all shame, guilt & hurt
No signs of suspicion, no early warning
Just a "Miss u All, "Love to All" note pinned to his shirt
Lying in the muddy dirt

Was he disabled, effeminate, impoverished
Was he obese, a nerd, a minority
Was he such an oddity
Whom which society labels Misunderstood, Misread, and Mislead
So shut inside the fury & pain engrained in his head
That in such fatality
He wanted release
By choosing to be a statistic, another casualty
Finality: he wanted peace

Misery's extremity
Adolescent apathy
The result from being bullied, one's disastrous entity
A terminal decree, fore incidentally...
Corey is he, she, you & me!

Perpetual tragedy
Little boy lost, child interrupted
The shock of a community
The bells of St. Augustine
The tears of a mother
As she buries her... Corey 16!

subway red

Waiting for you at Subway Red
Ceremoniously
Now is no longer my steam
Focus has fled, for I no longer have the breath to play dead
Redundantly
As if you live to scheme, and I sleep to dream

White chocolate fondue, such blak majik bewitches
I exhale, I disconnect (all of my self-respect)
So that you can imbrue
Within each bruise one's emptiness can cruise
Incoherent distraction
Helplessly
Convincing my respectability, you'd adopt some reciprocity
Chronic satisfaction, hidden within lies you ration
Effortlessly, I scramble, I race
Finding my wallet & keys-Putting on my IPod, flip-flops & my best face
To trek down avenues in search for you

Faction...
Self-denial, tonight's coming attraction
Subway Red
The tunnel its velocity discerns
Allays a lover's chivalrous melt, & yet slow to burn
I must have gluttony for punishment
Because to everyone's astound
I head trip, believing you no longer want me around
Then instantaneously you arrive, I come alive
Tears incessantly charts
Never once assessing the damage
Your baggage is doing to my heart

Cause it seems all we do is
Feast, fight, drink, drug, fuck, & cuss
You take the train, I on the bus
The moment the conductor slams the door
That's the end of us... "Temporarily"!

Yet still I wait, by the phone, your home & my computer
Foolishly
Praying for a call, email or even a text
Depressing when stressing over a fucking loser
Because after sex, what's next...
My clairvoyant contentment
(Never mind my heart's growing resentment)
This isn't fair
Because you & I know, one can never be a pair
But of course, I'm just taking all this shit out of context

Our affair's at a decline
Yet I still make it to the train on time
And you shall know me by the queer tone buried beneath my baritone,
the flirt in my stroll & the scent of my cologne
Sea of voices, an ocean of faces, anticipation builds, anguish races
I am threshed with meager trinkets your guilt gifts affords
I'm elated, can't you tell by the butterflies my belly-zone accords
2nd page, we engage cafe avenues, Moonlight rendezvous
Hugs & Kisses shower, all I want is forever
Yet you can only stay for an hour

Magnolia Bouquets
Their petals are blindingly wilting away
Passion's paradigm
I lay drenched beneath sorrow's stench, time after time
On the level, no use in trusting a try
For it has now come down to a "Do or Die" for you & I

Subway Blue: And there's still no sign of you
Subway Green: The voice of reason, a season unknown & unseen
Subway Yellow: Making love to Romeo, Casanova & his cousin Othello
Subway Orange & purple: Catastrophic circumstance, hurdle after hurdle
Subway Black: Happy Hour Whore's extraction ...yet I keep coming back

Lounge in one's sentimental soin
Our manifesto's plebeian
Still I make pilgrimage to the sweet of its sin
Seasonal stir
Chilling after effects, a misdirection the heart transfers
Hand to mouth, skilled in pair
Please kill the thrill that returns me to you over & over again
Free me from you, Damn-it... "I'M BEGGING YOU"!
You can even text-it- Just hurry...
Before we reach the next exit!

ragtime

Pack up the pictures
Delete the texts & e-mails (every single one)
Breakaway from memory's embrace
By erasing his face from the pages of your facebook, twitter & myspace
Pry into your pride, resurrect its potency
Hey, love whore, he doesn't want you anymore
So what the hell you still hangin on for

Strip out misery's mesh
Wash your heart, wipe up your tears
Face the ugly hiding in your mirror, it's dutiful
To shatter insecurity's inseam, then stand proud and scream
"Bitch you are beautiful"!!!!
Now go on...Don't be a hypocrite, swallow denial,
digest his lies, then realize
It's been more than a year since he said goodbye

Let go of all the anger, jealousy, confusion, bitterness
And layers & layers & layers & layers of emptiness
The breath that keeps wishing him death
Will be the same tongue that digs your own grave
Bear no acts of mayhem or malice
Psychotic antics, disrespectful threats
Merely because you're enchained to hurt, frustration & neglect
Retract... and as a matter of fact, stop wearing all black
For none of this shit will bring him back

By the way, stop trying to forge a friendship with his family & friends
You know they never liked your ass from the get
In fact... "Who did you think was spreading all y'all shit"?
Allow forgiveness to even the score, by finally letting go
And learning to love yourself a little more
Kicked in the gut, tossed to the dirt-True, a break-up hurts
But it's up to you to dust it off your skirt

Regurgitate
All of his pathetic promises
(Not to mention your self-hate)
Exfoliate, a life's at stake-Hurry, time won't wait
And your intervention's not up for negotiation nor debate
Do you really think he's sitting at home
Thumbing through guilt's anthology
What will it take for you to move on
A sympathy fuck & a formal apology

How many ways can your soul suffer
How many drinks can your blood consume
You saw the writing on the wall-In fact, you helped to write it
But didn't think it'd fall
Well it did, so get over it!

and he runs

And he runs
& why not, he's a pro & a hoe
Our love's a gun
Buried to a rot-It plots
Misery's empathy, (you'll find me) 3rd row
And he runs
To bosom his fears
Bruised & flawed-His lies inherently thawed
My wishful thinking & an ocean of tears
Confusion thumbs
True, it was me that decreed... "Jeffrey, I hate you"!
But it was never a motive to chase you away
Nor a ploy to bait you

I took a chance
And almost instantly, you manipulated my mind
2 drinks per dance
Boy-Bewitched-After which, the mutilation of his pride
Out of sight, out of mind
What I don't know won't hurt
Voyage unto an emotional enterprise, my prize: Another heart hazard
Secrets uncovered, deception sobers
So as his arrogant exit shoulders
Let us all hail the pompous bastard

And he runs
But hey, you do that when you're scared & strife
Despair's a crippling scheme
Insecurity drums-I succumb, growing incoherently numb
Watching beauty's knife
Castrate every dream
While confiscating the breath out my life

And he runs
A malicious fate
Because he was weak all along
No recon ciliated debate
No cheap thrills, No free refills. No romantic Re-Runs
Just back to that black "Hick-Dick"
Where he belongs

And he runs
As if a matter of life & death
A behavior unbeknownst to me
Unfamiliar tongues-Look what we've become
I'm gasping, at least let me catch my breath
Envy's epitome-"Damn it" just tell me where, in our affair
Did you decide to decree, "Cel bacy's Clemency"...
And get so much damn energy

Hatred's a cloak
Who kicked me in the gut, grabbed me by the throat
I'm clouded by consequence
Surrounded in a cloud of smoke
Insecure trails-Yet my longing inhales
1,528 mile choke
Tears talcum, panic ignites
Shortage of vodka & Valium, the increasing of paranoiac parasites
Complex & Confused
Torch poems, sex clones
Midwest Muthfucka's blues
Stews while bitterness picks to lick over my bones

Forgive my stupitdity
Excuse the excessiveness lounging inside my emptiness
That of which allowed you to fuck with me
But I'm insecure, and I can't help it
See what you're absence is now doing to me
I'm a man-A Blaque gay man in love
And to which such desperation gives

I'll forgive & mend…
I'll forgive your punk stunts
I'll send "Forget Me Nots" & "Love Me Do's"
Do whatever you want
I'll pray religiously-Even vow to endow total celibacy
Compromise to shit you know as well as I, I despise
Nothing's to improbable nor impossible
If all of this would bliss, granting me one more kiss
One that would lead me back to you

Atonement: The goodbye hysterics
Au revoir Anari, Adios Anari, Arrivederci' Anari…
Well, when will men stop running away from Anari

And he runs
As I've now grown old & tired of chasing
I'm tossing my guns
For vengeance is now worth embracing
Maybe before my flight lands
He'll be there waiting
This time with his heart in hand & both wedding bands
Ready to settle his soul
Into the life that we once planned
And stop all this god-damned running
"Please Jeffrey…Stop running"!

and I run

And I run...
Jumping through tears
Leaping over lies
Crashing into memories, sexin enemies
All of whom I ultimately despise

I'm running...
Blindingly bumping into my yester years
Soaring fearlessly eagle-free
Boundless surrender, I move swiftly
From mild to wild, this Starchild
Racing shamelessly

I'm running...
Hopping over homeless skids, gun-toting kids
Pimps & priests, beauty & their beasts
Political hypocrites, constituent illiterates
I accelerate, defying the limits of my pride
Cause the loneliness I feel inside
Could disintegrate our fate & outrun the sky

From...
Downtown to Korea town, Lynwood to Hollywood
Paris to Kansas, New England to New York, Prague, Berlin
Beneath the ancient ruins of Rome, between the plains in Spain
To the rooftop of my Mother's home
A southern Church house, to every God-damned bathhouse
Subways, to trains, forests & their desert lain
Cabs, bus, a one-way ticket, I picket... "Love or bust"!
Air flights, gay websites, club nightlife
City, state, continent to country
North, south, east & west,
The sands of our past, stain to stale the hourglass
Misery's aftermath, link one lie your vows endowed
Curtains cry, fountains dry, if nothing less

I'm running...
Hoping to run into our past
Cheat the clock, hole in my left sock
I grunt, I gasp, as I tirelessly slump
The race isn't won... (What, do I look like Forrest Gump?)
My lungs wept, ("heh") I can't take another step
And yet, this restless heart
Rapidly regrets-Dying for some spec of air
Inhale the laws of a sensitive male
And pray that you're still living in there
My shrink says Anari, you're mentally unstable
Your skin is no longer thick, you're dysfunctional
& you're past 36
You're out of touch, because you're over weight
And you drink too damn much
Take it easy or I'ma have to prescribe total soul sobriety
Well fuck that, this & him too
Rehab, "My Ass"!-Die, I'll gladly try!
If I can no longer have you
Scouting naked in a rainstorm
Hailing of thunder-Nocturnal earthquakes
You see our love was not the norm
Sweet addiction
Like Cocaine's infliction in a cup of Cornflakes

I'm running...
For it was something magical about our one night stand
One touch left your smile in my eyes
& 6 fairies in my right hand
Where in God's name could you be
Was my love that much of a threat
That you'd up and hide from me
I've searched everywhere...
Restaurants, churches, theatres, beaches, concerts, museums,
West Hollywood gyms, bathhouses, schools,

Hospital clinics, heaven & hell, jail cells
Shit even the goddamned courtroom
This final frame is crucial, my Queer fears is now a Boom
Cause I'm the wedding band without his groom

A phoenix with no wings-Confusion's rye, I sigh
Cause though miracles pinnacle... They still need wings to fly
I, the accused-For my love, you irreversibly excused
Bargain sorrows unfurled
I discontent-Peeling away a drunken dismay
Feeling pathetic & naked to the world

Contemplate all the passion Fueling my need
Lubricate vanilla whispers feeding my feed
Penetrate cinnamon shadows guiding love's lead
6 Zinfandel sips-48 thrusts-2 tongues
1 Irish sprung-The other black & submissively hung
A synchronization of queer fate-"But Wait"...
The memory still stews
But will its beauty brew a "The End" for "Me & U"?

I'm running...
For our affair is ending
So I've no time to skip, cruise, pace or jog
I've gotta do something
Since reading about our breakup in your myspace, facebook & twitter
blogs
Darkness sheets
I, the insomniac whom stirs, while the town's asleep
Drinks after drinks until my tears leak
The fittest of the purest-"Godspeed", to thee who endureth
Perspective pleats-An agonizing defeat
Though I know tomorrow, the saga repeats
Reconciliation's quest-I'll score-"A personal best"
Until that thrill, I'll still be...
"Shit, you know the rest"!

marshmallow boy

Marshmallow boy ~ Sepia-Cellophane lips
The filth they exhume ~ Ahoy, the lies they employ
Marshmallow boy ~ Confectionery wit
Campaign illicit doom ~ Rationing from out your left tit

Marshmallow boy ~ Tangerine tears
Circa Lavender groom ~ You mischievously appear, year after year
Marshmallow Boy ~ No need to act so pseudo-pristine
Your deception is in full bloom ~ Indeed, a good read
Back in a 1945 Blue-Boy magazine
(Behind the Hollywood Canteen)

Saturated thirst
Caged in confusion's curse
Undo your girth
Blindfold my soul to rape his earth
Marshmallow boy, Marshmallow Boy!

How you wish you could crust
Crucify fascist inclinations administering youth & lust
Dying to get at least one of us to trust
Oh the thrill, such a shill to consume
Tastings of self-deceit & marmalade perfume
One lick and your boom's doomed
Marshmallow boy, Marshmallow Boy!

Marshmallow boy ~ Delinquent, degenerate
Catholic decoy ~ Circumspect a leather bear's toy
Marshmallow boy ~ Veteran militant
A wealth of joy ~ Though 62 & still unemployed

Marshmallow boy ~ Aged, staled & sinking
Blame nostalgia's shame & the cheap vodka you're drinking
You're at a loss, shacked up in no where's land
Selling off your Circa-B.S. (Bullshit)
At all costs to the evolution of man

A kaleidoscope of desire
Mr. Hypocrite never to rationalize, realize, never dare to retire
Cause you're so busy stealing fables, & irons out of the fire
It's not enough that you have a need to be heard
It'll never be enough, because you also gotta have the last word
Marshmallow boy, Marshmallow Boy!

Disastrous circumstance, a mandated default
This is the life you've vexed & oversexed from out virility's vault
Still it's time to relinquish your geriatric stance
No use in acting innocent, shy or coy, just sit back, relax & enjoy
Your yesteryears revered...Marshmallow boy, Marshmallow Boy!

gypsy mama blaque

Gypsy mama blaque
I think it's about that time
To tell today's "Boy Boom", of my doom (U Groomed)
At "World's Fair" New York City
Back in the summer of 1929
Anchor's away, Anchor's ahoy
Salute your Time Square's sailor boy
Carting a sack of hopes, dreams, innocence & youth
And to tell you the truth
I only wanted to be a star, but never by far a ham
Yet, the studios never held auditions
To cast their next leading "Lavender Man"

Swept up in a time of decadence & sheer delight
Champagne thrills spill across Sennett's 6minute movie reels
Intoxicated by the scent of white nights, bright lights
Radio land airwaves, red carpet stairways
Prohibition's commission, Sleazy speakeasies
There you'll find behind the "St. Francis Hotel"
Suite #316, "Arbuckle & Rappe's" adjoining room
Oh, the scandal stardom can consume
Openings, premieres, debuts
Flappers & Tux, Pickfair pin-ups, Stork club's pub
All there to toast a Vaudevillian's Revue
Now a wash-out, somehow washed-up

And then there was you, My sweet...
Gypsy Mama Blaque
Give me my life back
My life, when I was young, handsome & hung
A dish fit for the screen & stage
Instead, I'm now aged
Incontinent, bitter & enraged

Whisked away in my solemn seclusion
70 years ago to this day
And hey, I'm still waiting for my conclusion...

Gypsy mama Blaque
The lies of a fortune teller
With eyes of Helen Keller
You bewitched me
I was dumbstruck... "DumbFuck"!
The shop boy who makes good, you swore I would
You foretold fame, beauty & all its riches
I wagered all I owned
And with a flick of a coin, I sold to you my soul
Now those days of the golden age are long gone...
And I wanna be done!!!

world's fair (carnivale)

Come to the Wold's Fair
A circus filled with games, crimes, prizes & all other shady surprises
Feast on atomic o zones, found in Hot Dogs, Popcorn, Peanuts,
Cell phones & Cotton Candied Ice-cream cones
You'll be amazed at the many wonders that await you
Take a ride inside tunnels whom funnel fear, greed & valor
From triumphs to tragedies
There's fun & guns for everyone, so bring the whole family
Step right up, let me direct you to the left
You'll see in this ring we have...

Reality shows, Pop culture hoes, Crime time-Prime time portfolios,
Diet & Yoga infomercials, Back lot-Big Top, White lies & Negro Spirituals,
Diabolical democracies, Marital atrocities, Child custody & Life insurance
policies, Global warming, Militant vigilante, Police brutality,
Prejudicial constitution, egregious prosecution, Racketeering ring,
Child prostitution, Religion's occult, Peta's revolt, Chronic paranoia,
Rampant homophobia, Bugs, Woody & Daffy, Crunch Berries &
Salt-water taffy, Cancerous wares, HIV/Aids scare, Homeless families
residing everywhere, SSI & Unemployment census, Crack-Pipe dreams,
Methamphetamine fiends, Hot Dogs-Gumdrops-Cookies-Vodka
Lemonade, Black Swan, Opium angels, "A Star is Born" on the hit parade,
State's bankruptcy, Adult illiteracy, Hostage takers, Mover & shakers,
Lullabies & Carousels, Our juvenile males cramped inside
Over-populated prison cells, Senior living overrated-oversold,
School Bully patrol, Serial rapists & Killers up for early parole, Humility's
demise, Fatality's enterprise, Mis education of youth & how it reaches him
The sins of a Priest & how he preaches them, Veggie burgers-Soy water,
Father 1 molesting his 2nd son & only daughter, Philanderers,
Philanthropists, Atheist & Buddhists, College tuition, Cosmetic
transplants, America's obesity, Healthcare-Health Scare, Remuneration's
Mutilation, Opera, Salsa, Reggaton,(mama I've seen enough, can we
please go home..."No"!) Gospel choirs, Jazzy big bands, Rock & Roll Soul,
Grandma's hands, Basquait, Warhol, Van Gogh, Picasso, Stravinsky &

Michelangelo, Gershwin, Bach & Arlen, The Renaissance of Harlem, Gothic musings, Lip, nipple, tongue & ear piercings, Pop culture, Black Friday vultures, Lothario Impresarios, Gym junkies, Celebrity flunkies, CD'S, BLUE-RAY DVD'S, IPODS-IPADS & IPHONES, Al Capone & his chaperones, Bath Salts, Rock gardens, Environmentalists, Animal rights activists, Teresa, Mandela, Ghandi, Earthquakes, Thunderstorms, bombs over Tsunami, Sports buff, Computer Geek, British invasion, Indian Reservation, European & Asian immigration, Facebook fascination, an Insurgent's assassination, Daunting Diva, Drunken Poet, Ailey, Graham, Fosse, Dunham, Silent movie theaters, Tuesday's double feature, Cabin in the sky, Stormy Weather, Missile ships, the sun's eclipse...

Barter scales of good & evil-its pendulum garters the wages of sin
Using Illuminati's candy to lure you in
A terminal thirst, should you feed on its curse
But first, I implore-Look to your right, for there's more...

Castles & Cathedrals, Villains & Heroes, Faieries, Elves, Birds, flowers, Ancient ruins, Sacred Showers, dissolution, air pollution, Beguine's spin, Ziegfeld follies, The decadence of Berlin, Social entity, aligns one's badge of identity, Freedom march, St. Valentine's day massacre,
Bloody Sunday-Yesterday-Today-Tomorrow & any thereafter, Pedophilia, Necrophilia, Child prodigy, "Don't ask-Don't Tell's" policy, Vietnam vets, Panther party, Gay Holocaust, Wilde, Isherwood, Hughes, And the many "LGBT'S who've more than paid their dues, Stonewall riots, Governmental gimmicks, Pharmaceutical highs, Teenage suicide, Stock market crash, Minimum wage feeding on stale bread & tuna hash, Terrorist threats, Cultural debate, Nuclear war's resounding fate, Deposition's turmoil-Proposition 8, Self-Righteous iberals, Political ineffectual shacked up with Down Low Bisexuals, World leaders trampling all over their shady bottom feeders, Gangland packets, Psycho-analysts prescribing anti-depressants & strait jackets, a prayer for England, donations for Africa, depravity is universal, yet the deeper we examine-Greed continuously feasts off another's famine, Cargo shorts-flip flops, cocaine blondes & dred locks selling "Happy Shots" down at your local Hemp shops, news, press, paparazzi, gossip columnists' venom, all their slanderous scandal you can read in em, mafia menage, spy espionage, Satanic music,

Freedom of choice-Freedom of Art, never mind the many who have died from worshiping your art, Spiritual Karma, GED'S, EBT'S, Sugar-Daddies, Baby mamas, Nomadic transient, your next door neighbor always wanting a favor, Asylum's resort, Einstein's find & Kinsey's report, Stardust, Moon glow, Daou's Serenade, Nickelodeon's arcade, Judy's Somewhere over the rainbow, Conservative fundamentals, Democratic & Republican differentials, King's speech, KKK'S Outreach, Mad cow disease, Drill platoons, Soul Train, Kung Fu & and my favorite Saturday morning cartoons, Time square, Lady liberty, Wuthering heights, Vaudeville, Faberge', Burlesque, Cabaret, Sex spas, karaoke bars, sleazy dives, casting couch, swinger sets, WWF, Pimps & Hoes, Gypsy pirates & UFO's, Racial profiling, Weaves & perms, Chaos-Corruption, Self-preservation-self destruction, Time vs. chance & through all this circumstance...
The State of the world, budgeted to an anguishing deficit

And no matter how you look at it
It seems to have lost its paradigm, angles, circles & lines
(Not to mention, Rhythm's Rhyme)
Hope, Peace & Respect now has succumbed to a low ebb
Clowns make funny faces, to rob your worth leaving no traces
Elephants, Lions, tigers, monkeys & bears
Have all been stolen from their home's habitat
Slaves trained, to do death defying feats,
To keep you on the edge of your seat, to entertain
So are they to blame should they rebel, should they heinously attack
You'll be mystified, terrified & at times even horrified
Watching animated images who border chaos & disorder
Life's strife & Death...Yet, if I'm permitted to catch my breath

Come to the world's fair
Sign over your soul if you dare
Pay to get in, pray to get out
And if you do... Good for you
If not, do come back & see us again
(Oh, & don't forget to bring a friend)!!!

he had it comin...

Open up Case File: # 053201783
Decadence, Debauchery, & Deception...1921
Hippodrome Theatre, Baltimore-That's where I first met Joe
A Vaudevillian comic with a salacious talent for making people laugh
Needless to say I, a "Lavender Arabesque" (in the follies & burlesque) fell
from first glance-So in fact... "We COMBINED OUR ACT'!
Now what Joe didn't tell me was that aside from his love of the stage he
was also a raving alcoholic whom seemed to take pleasure in beating his
lovers into total submission.
Well, after years & years of black eyes, broken ribs, swollen lips, I don't
mean to be flip... But I didn't find Joe so funny anymore
I guess you could say I'd had my fill, of being 3rd rate on his playbill
And besides from being constantly beaten-up, the act was long
Washed-up-So with "Bags packed, a new act, New York lights,
Minsky's theatre, vintage vengeance on opening night"!
"Light's down, curtain's up, a hush rushes to a roar, and what's more...
Joe's bloody body lays stabbed center stage 2 feet from the orchestra
floor-"Hmm, seems my debut.. "OPENED TO RAVE REVIEWS"!

He had it comin-The Good-4-Nuthin
So I suggest you watch where you put the blame
No circumspect, his disrespect
Surely should count for somethin
Don't say you wouldn't have done the same

Open up Case File: # 066327218
"Oh Father"...1962
I was 15, an altar boy at the neighborhood church
You know, a good little Catholic kid
Born & raised in the New Jersey skids
That's where I met Father "Man of the Cloth"!
He was religious, neighborly & trusting-A Father-Figure you might say
Always knew how to make all the boys smile & obey
Unbeknownst to me that all the while
Father "Man of the Cloth" was an adroit pedophile

And oh how he loved watching me kneel to pray
So right after Sunday's service, when he cornered me in the parish
The first thing I recalled was being touched inappropriately
The grabbing of St. Helen's Rosary, the tears of my mother
"Oh Father", forgive me for I have sinned
But with all respects to Ms. Tilly divine...
"The razor blade slit his throat just fine"!

He had it comin-The Good-4-Nuthin
So I suggest you watch where you put the blame
No circumspect, his disrespect
Surely should count for somethin
Don't say you wouldn't have done the same

Open up Case File: # 086532159
Til Death due Us Part...1985
Charlie was a "Hottie", an avid party-boy
The most "GO TO PIECE OF ASS"...
To ever pass throughout the lains of San Francisco
An era of sex, drugs & disco
Alleys, piers, underground bath houses & Pre-condom pornography
Yeah, Charlie was wild with a weakness for anyone & everything
Til one morning's visit to the local county clinic
"Dr. Diagnosis" answer, "Hey Mr. Hedonistic Dancer...
"You've now got the "GAY CANCER"!
Charlie was so elated that he decided he'd come home and share the news with me
A vow to always love, honor & protect me
But never when he was fucking me
"Well, it's been 6years now since Charlie's death
& I'm now dating a man by the name of HIV"!

He had it comin-The Good-4-Nuthin
So I suggest you watch where you put the blame
No circumspect, his disrespect
Surely should count for somethin
Don't say you wouldn't have done the same

Open up Case File: # 001864471
Crime of passion...2006
My man Ian was quite a "DISH"!
Strong, sexy, rich & everybody wanted a taste of his "SHHH"!
His swagger was fire, his swipe was ripe.
Rough, raunchy, tough, tight & could take it all night.
Yup, Ian was simply Anari's type.
But it seems that Ian didn't identify himself as straight or gay
His philosophy of monogamy was screwing anyone who landed on his dick
(Y'all know how those "DOWN-LOW HOE'S" like to play)
A lover scorned
& after finding out about his 3rd wife giving life to his 2nd born
It was then & there I remembered
Something my mommie told me when I was little boy...
"You've gotta let a man be a man"!
And so I did, when I shot him 6 times in the head, while he slept...
"IN A BURNING BED"!!!

He had it comin-The Good-4-Nuthin
So I suggest you watch where you put the blame
No circumspect, but his disrespect
Surely should count for somethin
Which is why, I'm sure you would've done the same!

Open up Case # 042869011
Revenge of the Gay Bashed...2012
Due to the pending appeal, and the age of the criminal
This case has been declared... "CONFIDENTIAL"!

"Gentlemen, having been found guilty by a jury of your peers
You are hereby sentenced to death by electrocution...
"MAY GOD HAVE MERCY ON YOUR SOULS"
"I guess we had it comin"!

ham

Greetings gents & grooms
After that lovely feast of oyster stew, pheasant, clams & yams
Might we adjourn to the Gloucester pub or the billiard room
To ooze over cigars and bourbon booze
A topic to gossip...Let's allow our idiosyncrasies choose
Oh, don't let me be a ham

A fateful recall
Yet, I must admit that I had a ball
Playing Miss Chatelaine at Erasmus hall..."Oh, don't let me be a ham"!
Funny thing this evening I should read in the stars
That Atlantis will soon collide with Mars
To give race relations to humanity & Poseidon's Quasar...
"Oh, don't let me be a ham"!

Well, being the forthright man that I am
I heard that a gentleman farmer living in Siam
Made a fortune off wet whiskey & dry jam...
"Oh please, don't let me be a ham"!
Sophisticated nemesis
Dare I experiment-With such queer merriment
Excuse me, but we don't allow sloth & snobbery on the premises
Only slaves whom rave republican sentiment...
"Oh, don't let me be a ham"!

And on a more redundant take
How rude of Mr. Mc Kan, & to think I was a devoted fan
He ditched his date, to dine with a Nigerian ape...
"Oh don't let me be a ham"!
Poor, poor Geena Bleu, I hear she's being sued
For having such a gay attitude
And for mispronouncing the word "Bienvenue"...
"Oh, don't let me be a ham"!

Catch the dish straight from Ms. Stanwyck's Valet
All hail Mr. Parfait
He drank himself to death, while his wife attended Balanchine's ballet...
"Oh, don't let me be a ham"!
Respect to the cruel fools & their crass
But please be sure to subscribe to the new law passed
Pastors & Priests chasing after adolescent ass
Will be justifiably reprimanded ("I know, y'all can't stand it)...
"Oh, don't let me be a ham"!

A toast, to our aristocracies of arrogance, ignorance & greed
May you all have so little of what you want
And so much more of what you need
Taunt your flaunt while yet your heart still starves
"Darling, not now, the pheasant has yet to be carved"!
"Oh, don't let me be a ham"!

Well then, can you beat such a despicable void
The dish, is that somewhere down in Illinois
I can still eat catfish & grits, after 6 weeks of being unemployed
"Oh, don't let me be a ham"!
Pardon me, though I don't mean to boast or brag
But I was a stalwart at the cathedral choir in Singapore
While doing the Black-Bottom & the Michigan Rag
Need I say more... But an..."OUCH", to that darn splinter
I got while doing the Charleston with "Sir Chaplin"
Back in 1942 late December... 'Oh, don't let me be a ham"!

Yesterday while sipping on a vodka malt
I heard that Same-Sex marriages will one day exalt
No more senseless murders & assaults- "Honey hush, & pass the salt"!
"Oh, don't let me be a ham"!
Rumor has it that Prohibition's power
Will shrivel away like the petals of a honeysuckle flower
And our "Ladies of the Night"
Will start to charge by their worth instead of by the hour...
"Oh, don't let me be a ham"!

The Diva Daou is shell-shocked
She sopped her slop, burned her mop, closed up shop
And don't you find it peculiar
No one dared thought to question her maid, butler or bellhop...
"Oh, don't let me be a ham"!
For shame Mr. & Mrs. Uptight
I found it deliciously impolite
That they chose to fight, at "PICKFAIR'S opening night...
"Oh, don't let me be a ham"!

The stigmas & hypocrisy of man, is now a flash in the pan
I uncovered such revelation while reading Photoplay & Lifestyles
Confidential in the can
Clam, Sham..."BOOM, BAM"!
And now thanks to this poem, I'll be another man out on the lam
I bid you farewell my friends-But before I end
"PLAY IT AGAIN SAM"... And don't let me be a ham!!!!!

Kid (dedicated to Sir Chaplin)

As I sit stoned in age
Sweet ubiquity, in all of its antiquity
Gracefully insulated in my regale
Conditioned to a fictitious splendor
Its decadence haunts
Dowdy in grace
Slowly glowing dim across a winter's ember
Yet, I am commissioned
Held captive by your perpetuated fate
That even now in my fugue state
I can deliciously remember

The age of vaudeville, the year of the flapper
Their apparitions dancing abandonedly across my memories
Embellishing echoes of an era lost, our forgotten romance
Preserved, stored somewhere in time
I too, have seen that movie back in 1904
Clandestinely inclined from first glance
When faces implored porcelain portraits, a beauty unknown before
Vintage tinsel, such cinematic grandeur, I'm cloaked in its debris
Enslaved to its soundtrack, though I know you're never coming back
Yes, I was bewitched, knocked silly
Intoxicated by a wondrous idolatry-Fore it was in my dunce
I loved you once-This kid, the ID

All that remains now are movie reels, Ziegfield Playbills
Screen life, Gossip life about Hollywood life & all its glamorous trife
Theatrical Scandals, photoplay magazines, communistic scripts,
Contractual limos, meals, jewels, beaded costumes bunked in trunks
Chaplin, Haines, Keaton, Chaney, Fields, Gilbert, Barrymore
Astor, Loy, Gish, Bara, Brooks, Arbuckle, the Pickford's & Marx's Bros.
Swanson, Bow, Harlow, Garbo, Dietrich, Baker, Navarro & oh…
"Mr. Valentino"! ☺

Chipped autographs strewn across cracked Sepia photographs
I scan these wrinkled hands across our what-if's & what-used-to-be's
And for just a moment away from my life & his modern misery...
Ah, the roaring 20's-Her sweet rendezvous coos, from satire to slapstick
Hold my breath, closing my eyes-I sigh, I fly, as I again am there with you

Inseparably we
Wrong or right, day or night, my eyes only rhapsodize
The instant they colorize, seeing our story glory digitize in black & white
A consequential visual, still I welcome their imagery & residuals
Epilogue:
We were Gods, legends... Stars
No curtain calls needed now, as we have taken our last bow
Just a toast, might I propose
Here's to you, all of the silent screen actors everywhere
I salute you...The end of a love affair!!!

torch song

I'm mad about the boy
My average Joe-My only joy
Don't steal me away, for I'll never go
My life is by his side
He's all I know

Entranced, enraptured
Like Pompeian cathedrals surrounding a Sardinian Savoy
I'm compelled, so you could never bewitch me from his spell
Fore my soul he controls
I submit-My darling Joe

Stardust & Ocean's glow
He is my heart's whisperer, my hero
I love him heaps, I am his for keeps
Though low on the dough, not well to do & yes...
He at times beats me too
Still his kisses are the sweetest of voodoo
Insatiably delicious, so not to seem cross or pretentious
But I'll not ask for the moon, I have the stars...And my Joe!

black winter

Interlude...Picture it, "Atlantic City" 1904
I'm sitting, wasting away by the docks, pitching teardrops
Wishing every wave, would (One Day) breakaway
And I'll see you-"The Love of my Life" once more
My black winter!

Black winter ~ Blue December
Ode to a love atoned ~ And all the lies your eyes chaperoned
Seasons shift~ Sorrow corridors
I never once imagined, all the damage, my heart could ever baggage
From getting sore over you not wanting me anymore

Black winter ~ The instant you entered
Passion was the play & its epicenter
Yet today, you now act as if you don't remember
You cornered my lips to your kiss
And I flung my tongue to be swept inside its bliss
One touch, and a thousand fears allay to rest
Watching heaven's angel mangle between my breasts

And now the poison dissolves, as my need for you withdrawals
I sigh a dry heave, I can't breathe, oh the misery
This damn humidity
I thought outside the box, you pried the locks
Gave me emotional affectations & their aftershocks
Now look at what each one is doing to me

Black winter ~ One's Bi-polar member
Memoirs in the pale ~ Simmering in the sweet & sour of my hell
I'm so impure, so unsure
This merciless overcast
Is more than one should endure
Like another stain to ingrain our hourglass

I can't shake this fate
I want out of this palace of pain & malice
This odious sensory reeking of lust & love's thievery
No solitude or sage for either page
Just a lonely spell to shell love's aromatherapy

Emptiness is restored
For my love for you is cancerous
A resentment employed, anguish toys, consequence implores
For my pride has long been destroyed
Like the curse of Lazarus, was it fair of you
To swear "True Blue", then "We Were Through"!
Before the 6th act scene 2…What did I ever do to you?

Flashbacks replay,
As my loneliness tries to shake loose from the noose
No inch of strength, it's so damn hot today
Plebeian & paltry
Well who the hell are you
To call our affair an infatuated adultery
None of this shit makes any sense
You knew from the start that my heart
Was insecure, inexperienced & intense

Though no whether the chills that spill
Let the clouds bed my head, let every thunder strike my plight
You were only having fun, and now I wish I had a gun
For I'd shoot U, Me & this God-Damned sun

The birth of a dream
So unresolved & so unredeemed
Though no matter the tears I jazz
I smile, knowing all the while
This black winter too shall pass

rasputin

What have I done to make you hate me so
Why, are your only thoughts of me
Scales between ecstasy's epitome & your personal lavatory
Imprisoned by love's thievery
I can't let go, so I'll never break free

You're sarcastic & frugal
A filthy obnoxious mongrel
Yet my body subdues to your sweet torture
It resolves, soothes my addictive withdrawals
Rips me out of my drawers... (And I love it, I love it)

You're a painstaking lie
Still I fester in each muscle you flex-To next, wake up in a pigsty
I'm thrilled to your spell, quenched beneath an oasis of hell
You confuse my quandary
Like mixing dry cleaning in with wash laundry
You belittle, you berate-You pimp, you titillate
You tear at the very fabric of my esteem
I suffer kisses from another, I prostitute my pride-I succumb, I thrill
I overkill

You bait me with meager guilt-gifts
Merely for my suspicions to climb down
And my legs to lift
You see, you've stolen my bougina & life
You've injected your smile-Now I'm conflicted from its strife
Your kiss is cocaine-Addicting my lust & trust
Too cheap to spare a spec of tenderness
A portrait of evil-Celluloid of conceit
Wrapped up in the arms of emptiness
And though I surrender to an uttered defeat, I must repeat...
(I love it, I love it)

Why do I worship the worthless-Why am I so in love with hate
To want who I can't have-To have who I don't want
Is the same as slurping turpentine off a copper plate
Mr. Mistress embroiders my nightgown
As you play your Hoe-card, Suck dicks, just for kicks
Then Mannequin monogarry the minute I come around
My heart sirens and still you play deaf to its cry
Your sex is voodoo
Deny me of its high, and I'll surely die
You are my Casanova, Uriah Heap, my weakening infusion
I can't shake you, my grunge dodger
My Rasputin!

nutcracker (dedicated to Ms. Stanwyck)

I told you how important it was for you to never leave me
I explained it over & over
Why it was necessary that you remain in my life, Didn't I?
Yet in a moment's huff, you spit & spewed "Tough"!
A direct disrespect to my pride & my bluff
Now she's dead
As I'm now going to the chair
Her life forever bleeding in your hands
Yep, I guess all in love is fair

Bombarded with guilt & shame
Enchained to a love, we dare not speak its name
Fatal romance
My, the scandal this will brink
An insidious link, screw the neighbors, what will your children think
Come, before the cops arrive...let me fix us both a drink
Cause on the level, she did have it comin
See, I can cope with a shag, but the ole bag called me a "Nigger-Fag"
Say listen, I'm not getting any bang out of this
My life is now at a loss
Slave-chained, mocked-up, locked-up & doubled dirty-crossed
I hope you're satisfied
Look at what your one lie has now done to my life
I'm ruined, sacrificially sufficed
This is not about jealousy or animosity
I never thought of you as a possession
Even as they were arresting me, I took full responsibility
I even asked for my last rites that same night

Consequential entity
Penitence: Death sentence
Circumstantial inevitability
I fell in love with a lie that never loved me!

seasick

Whoa, can somebody tell me...What the fuck did I just walk into
Was I punk'd, pranked, or (as usual) incoherently tanked
Was I that sewn up in the sensation
That I somehow misread the invitation
Because I could've swore from the boys on the flier
That this was supposed to be a "Hunk-Party"
Yet all I'm seeing are diva wanna-be's & anorexic bodies
Parlaying & Sashaying around this "Punk-Party"
Circulate, speculate, calculate & at some point summarily evaluate
Queenagers, convalescent even conservative queens
Star fucker sluts starving their zero size, so they can fraternize
With studio executives, manic-depressives
No matter how campy or excessive
Their lure, touching on dreams, all of which to achieve such a luxury
With or without facetiousness & fuckery
Those that would by all means disassemble the pride of a man
Feeding his circumstance
With steroidal stance, cancerous tans & yep, you guessed it...
Bad hair-color transplants

What's the deal...I'm getting nauseous
Utterly disgusted, from being disrupted, subjected to botox-bitches
Saddidy sissies acting high-post & prissy
OK so, what gives...What kind of social shin-dig is this
Power bottoms feigning as tops,
Flow-showing in Christian briefs & flip flops
Serving their swerve with shade, trying to come off as fresh hot trade
Frontin with voices sounding like their high off of lithium & helium
Looking like grunge hoes out to audition for the latest reality shows
on Here TV & Logo channels

While we're doing jello-shots, they're flooding me with head shots
Trying to be seen
Dying to centerfold on a stripper's pole & the next flex magazine
Even willing to tuck their dicks, to disrobe on Drag Race's episodes 2, 4 &
6

Not all eye candy is pleasing to the soul
And in case you didn't know, I don't dyke, so take a hike... "Video Hoe"!
You see, bleu taught strang on how to ration the skins
To educate, regulate, teach you boys how to be men
I'd catch a death from all of the plastic-faggots packing this atmosphere
Thank God they at least have a bar up in here
Cause before I sink, "Hey, bartender I'm gonna need a another drink
Before I get the hell up on outta here

Instead of queens & kings, I'm in the presence of fag-hags & meth-queens
HMPH, some soiree, more like an aquarium
Clogged with stuck-up trish with Hollywood dreams & big dicks
Shit, I'd have a better time
Quoting prose with beat-niks at the annual freak-nik
Instead of fishing for what I'm wishing, & all I'm getting is... Seasick!!!

apathy (eat my cl_t)

Fuck you...
I ain't yo niggah, boo, shorty, homie
Or yo "What it do"?
Because I can assure whatever's happenin
It won't be a "Me & U"!
What's crag-a-lackin?
Nuntin's broke that needs to be fixed
& I've told you time & time again
We ain't bumpin lips, hips, bouginas or dicks
So stop askin!!!

Truth to the heart I despise you, your crew, your style and it's steelo
And the only libido, I've got for your overly inflated ego
Is a 10inch needle..."POP"
Recognize
My caliber's not to be compromised or compartmentalized
I'm too old of a cat to be fucked by a pussy
Or D.L. Thugs, that just wanna bust a nut
All up in Anari's "Honey Butt"!
Love is life, & life is divine
So the apathy you map is a Faux-paus, a booby-trap
And all it can bring is emotional Armageddon
To this life of mine

No scrub, you gets no hug
So save your kiss, smelling like chronic shit & pig-piss
I'm SOOOO not gettin undressed, cause I'm SOOOO not impressed
By the gear you rock or the ghetto lothario you stock
Flossin in tanks, saggin jeans & droopy drawls
Showing off your nappy-ass pubic hair balls
(Nasty bastard, you make my skin crawl)
I'm even least amused
By the ride you stretch, the abs & biceps you flex
Or your reward points to Starbucks, the Gym, Swap Meet & H&M... Next...

I suggest you address a man of my standards
By his government name, & not your retarded South Central slang

I'm up on game, so I'm not to be swayed nor hyped
You get drunk & high
Then cry-You're not gay
You're just curious, in denial or incoherently BI
Which is why so many women end up another HIV statistic on
Iyanla or Dr. Phil's talk show, C'mon let's get realistic
Cornrows & tats, with stacks of Polaroids of Penis penitentiary
You'd better save em for that bitch that's funding your commissary
Sup?

Your mother must be turning cartwheels in her grave
Saying to herself..."Look at what the hell I don raised"!
Oh and by the way, you thought getting me drunk
Later on, I'd get you crunked
Well looka here punk...I'm allergic to the hood
So spare me all of your Ebonic junk

Call me stuck-up
90210, "Wanna-Be-White"-A cocktease... Oh, Please!
Merely because I won't defrost & season
To wet your appetite- "Na Ne, Na Ne, Na Na"!
Your eyes may water, your teeth may grit
But some of my "NA NA" you sho ain't gon get
I'm my own man-Phenomenal Me... "Understand"?
Can you feel what I'm saying, are you willing to stand on what I'm laying
Are you even remotely inclined to sense my essence & its eloquence
Consider yourself lucky, cause if I was a bitch
I'd tell all y'all to eat my cl_t!!! (Fo realz, hahaha)

my dik iz the lik

My Dik Iz The Lik
It can turn nuns into nymphos
Housewives into whores
A virgin into a porn-star
A pimp to a trick
Why…
Becauze My Dik Iz The Lik!

But if you still don't agree
Then ask some members in my family…

UK Dik
European Dik
Norwegian Dik
Puerto Rican Dik
Jamaican Dik
Caucasian Dik
Asian Dik
Brazilian Dik
Guatemalan Dik
Australian Dik
Armenian Dik
Belizean Dik
Argentinean Dik
Israel an Dik
Russian Dik
German Dik
Japanese Dik
Swahili Dik
Irish Dik
Italian Dik
Indian Dik
African Dik
Mexican Dik

Korean Dik
Samoan Dik
Ethiopian Dik
Venezuelan Dik
Romanian Dik
El Salvadoran dik
Swedish Dik
Pilipino Dik
Creole Dik
Zulu Dik
Palestinian Dik
Cuban Dik
Egyptian Dik
Columbian Dik

Worldwide or simply ringside
My Dik iz a celebrity
I'm seen on Videos, Sports shows, Talk shows, Reality shows
Red Carpet walk, Media portfolios, even health infomercials

The Bigger It gets-The Richer I get
The Thicker It gets-The deeper you'll wet
My Dik iz lethal
It's said to have fed the hungry
Redeemed the lost
Turn pussy-loving bro's into "Down-Low" hoes
Make Mommas fight their Daughters over me
Even Fem-Dykes strap on me (Prosthetic ally)
So you tell me…Who can refuse the stick
Cut or Uncut-SHH, "Don't interrupt" because….
My Dik Iz The Lik!

Still undecided….
Here, question some of my cousins
We're an anatomy united…

Oakland Dik
Texas Dik
Brooklyn Dik
Compton Dik
Southern Dik
Middle Eastern Dik
South American Dik
Canadian Dik
("Shit Even") Alaskan Dik
Jersey Dik
Chicago Dik
Frisco Dik
D.C. Dik
East L.A. Dik
South Central Dik
Ventura Dik
Redneck Dik
Metro Dik
Ghetto Dik
Penitentiary Dik
Industrial Dik
Corporate Dik
Catholic Dik
Baptist Dik
Jewish Dik
Buddha Dik
Viagra Dik
420 Dik
Meth Dik
Crack-Head Dik
Ecstasy Dik
H.I.V Dik
Pedophile Dik
Adolescent Dik
Convalescent Dik
S&M Dik
Cyber Dik

HipHop Dik
Rock/Pop Dik
Country Western Dik
Punk-Funk Dik
Cut/Uncut Dik
Pretty Dik
Ugly Dik
Fat Dik
Skinny Dik
Homeless Dik
Psycho Dik
"Whew"...That's alotta dik.
"I gotta stop this shyt. B-4 my own Dik gets jealous"!

"OOPS", I almost forgot, if by chance you didn't see your dick listed...

_____
(sign your dick here)

Now you too are the "LIK"!!!! ☺

valerie

Valerie
Urban Aloe age 23
So undeveloped & unsure
Ripe with nymph naivety

Valerie
Kitty Venus
The misconception of desire
She acquires the ferocity of the penis

Oh Valerie, sweet Valerie
Don't fall in love with me
I'm strictly dickly
So to quicken me, would only sicken me

Valerie, my darling Valerie
Stop misconstruing a fag's empathy
As an interlude to illegitimate intimacy
Recognize & hear me
This union-ship is solely built on friendship
I assure you there will be danger up ahead
If you keep insisting we'll end up in bed

Valerie
She strays her crave blindingly
Untamed, unashamed
Festering her toils in the soils of homosexuality

Valerie
No ounce of luxury, you shower upon me
To bust such forbidden lust
Will ever crust a fuck-fest for us

Oh Valerie, my pretentious Valerie
Stop falling in love with me
You wanna play, but I'll never game
You can stroke for broke
But I still won't be moaning your name

Valerie, Valerie
You're beautiful & sexy as hell-But Hell, so am I
I'm not confused, curious, in denial, or even Bi
I'll be your best girlfriend
Be the palm to calm your emotional whirlwinds
But resign to mind one's factual forte'-If I say I'm gay...
Then "God-Damn It, leave it that way"!

Stop pressing your breasts up against my chest
Stop trying to kiss my lips, hugging me inches below my hips
Stop with the pathetic accusations,
That I am weak, a coward, that I hate women, I'm afraid of women
That I'm a fascist, one who hasn't been saved or laid by a woman
Just stop, Stop, Stop... "I'm just not into women"!

And no,
I'm not Bitch-Bashing
I just don't want titties sitting pretty on my back
Though tell me this...is it the challenge you thrill
Or the rejection you fear
Umbilically exempting, its conquest is pragmatic & tempting
Yet still Valerie, you're barking up the wrong tree
Thinking we'll consummate, bare a child or walk in matrimony
We won't, so don't...My sweet Valerie!

misconceptions

I wake, work, sleep, dream, eat, drink, drug, club, lie, cry, justify, testify, cheat, want, need, strive, stress, struggle, hate, pray, fuck, complain, migraine, jog, write, fight, impress, suppress, love, live, exist, implore, deplore... "No More...What am I doing all this shit for?

When...
I've got 3 hundred voices living inside my head
Spinning me round & round, gun at my brain, incarcerated insanity
Sweet peace, I'm losing ground-Can't see the road, only its bend
I wanna drape these blinds, lose my life under my bed
And pray for self-torture to end

Somebody help me...When my up won't touch down
When my in is too scared to come out
When my rhythm bears no rhyme
Do I cheat the past, or simply run out of time

Everyone's preaching,
Screaming, yelling & telling me to buck-up, step-up, rise-up & be a man
So busy signifying, vocalizing yet never realizing
It's hard as hell at times just trying to be a man
Am I to be judged, will I fit-in
Confused about my place & where he stands on God's land
Stigmas & social-whirlwinds
I follicle frustratingly, expected to achieve, persevere, follow rules
And should I once rebel, I'm bashed, trashed & ridiculed
Well I say... "Fuck you"!

Why must a man always have to justify
His soul's interruption, his psychological corrosion
Branded, ostracized, as if I don't dare qualify, nor rectify
The imagery of me you advertise, crucify, disarm, even bask
So condescending,
Making fortunes off all my misunderstandings & misgivings

Mis educated, male-bashed
Constantly misconstruing the man behind the mask
As if I don't own the right to copy write my own life
Depleted & beyond defeated
Well I've had it with being the contrast
Your laws expects out my ass

I'm more than just the bone of Adam
I am more than just musk & a big dick
I am heart & mind, wanting a little peace & respect
And just so that we're absolutely clear on the subject...
I'm not whining
Just defining the measure of man, & what it feels like for him
When he's reached the point of giving all he can!

men-o-pause (diet)

So...
You want me to lower my voice, whenever I talk
You want me to butch my switch, at all times when I walk
You say the only way we can have sex
Is if I tighten my abs, flash my "Bubble Butt Ass"
And beef up my biceps
& what's worse, that if I gain even one pound...
"You're Out of this Town"!

This is appalling
When we're around your friends, you keep me under a microscopic eye
Because you can't afford to be embarrassed or humiliated should I brink
The moment I let my hair down or have even one goddamn drink
You want a whipping-boy to rid you of all the ex's from your past
And not only was I that missing link
I yielded to such despicable demands
Merely to say that I too, have a man... "Ya think"?

Is it a sin, to not want to walk around looking all sickly & rail-thin
To be society's guinea pig
A manufactured recreation to suit your desires
The world's at a mass hysteria
Falling to the airs of social-acceptance & anorexia
The eyes of beauty is a defacing epidemic
Oh the tragedy, oh the insanity
Though no superficial skepticism will you find stewing in my metabolism

If I'm hungry, "I'LL EAT"! If I'm dieting, "I'LL CHEAT"!
Faux, facades, veils & robes
So what, if I need a tub of Crisco in order to fit in my clothes
Meintoone... "I LOVE YOU ME"!

For the life of me, & never will I understand
Why a man's ideology of attraction & its conduct
Borders along the perimeters of a narcissistic by-product
When studies show
That not all beauty regimens & dietary pharmaceuticals
Aired across nudie magazines, reality shows, the red carpet, weight-loss
& every workout infomercial
Though temporarily commercialize, yet never will immortalize the skin
A profitable venture, a dehumanizing sin, But then again...
What about the many medicinals recalled
Because it's taken the lives of so many of y'all

I'm sure the men from the early 1900's are just turnin in their graves
By the way you all behave
Rough, Raunchy, Tough and tight,
Subsisting only on cigarettes, soy latte and 2 egg whites
Well whatever u do, just don't choke on such hype
Cause there's about 3 hundred more of "U" in this club tonight
Prosthetic vanity, pathological corrosion, 6 seconds til explosion

If I'm horny, I'll fuck
If I fuck with the likes of you, "Then I'm Shit of Luck"!
Faux, facades, veils & robes-I'm still in demand, and it shows
Meintoone... "I LOVE YOU ME"!

"And now ladies & gentlemen
It's time for a breakdown...
So what...
My weight fluctuates
So what...
My drinking (at times) puffs out my face & impairs my thinking
So what...
Your body is "HOT", too bad your self-worth & self-esteem is "NOT"!
So what...
Your boyfriend is muscular like you... "Mr. Suicide Watch X's 2"!
SO WHAT, SO WHAT, SO WHAT, SO FUCKIN WHAT!

Eat to live, don't live to eat-I always say, but hey
Everyone is entitled to at least one cheat day
So...
This poem goes out to all my middle-men, the everyday ordinary man
You know...
The one not too hulk, not too waif
The one who eats all the carbs piled upon his plate
The one with a pudge in his belly, cellulite in his jelly
The one who works out at his job more than the gym
The one who doesn't need superficial shit to resign nor define him
The one who isn't trying to bliss, by living like he's on shows like...
"The Kardashians & the A-LIST"!
The one who doesn't define his sex appeal, by his muscular build
the car he rides, or by how many ribs he can feel

Just bear in mind...
This is only my convictions, my belief
I'm not, and will never be one of your many anemic creatures
Who can only get nourishment off Lemon water & a lettuce leaf
I've done the suppressant pills, power-walks, Yoga & treadmills
Still, I'm an artist-I have zest & zeal
So I'll be damned If I'm gonna deny my womb of a good meal

Hate on you, "WHOOPS" you hatin on me
Merely cause I don't need any gimmicks to mimic
Nor men like you to validate me
Happiness is with self
& not some adhesive attachment to someone else
Loving and embracing you from within, it's a declaration for celebration
Not matter the skin you may presently be in
So save your sticks & stones, your shady uppity ass chaperones
And to what do I say to you & your clicks
That the only way we can bump dicks, is if I'm fit in a size 6
Faux, facades, veils & robes- ᶠ you had a meal that was hearty & yummy
Lift up your shirt, rub you tummy and say...
Meintoone... "I LOVE YOU ME"!!!

my ashes (have u seen them)

Where is everybody going
Why is everyone rushing, and where are they rushing off to
I search in disparity, no longer able to see familiarity
Laughter's dissolving, faces decaying
Silence thickens the room, the party resumes
Yet no one's staying
A rainbow's spray now arrays shades of Grey
I touch their skin-So frail-So pale-So cold
As one by one they're steadily slipping away

Lifeless beauty
Here lying, writhing in pain
I try to suckle its hold, by trying to cradle their soul
Yet inevitably, fatality contains
Echoes of the past amass
My how translucently they spin
Traces of their lineage in its final grasp
Relinquish, to inherently enchain the wind

I crutch, I gut
Fore there's a hole inside of me
I fill with Chardonnay wine and bittersweet memories
The stench of your death permeates my heart
And no matter a smile the clown shows
When the lights drown, and no one's around
I fall apart

Have you seen my ashes
Where, oh where have they gone
I've searched frantically everywhere, from coffin to urn
Yet with each passing day, not a trace
I simmer, stew, burn, discern
Because they've yet to resurface, & I'm afraid they won't return

Where is everybody going
Why didn't someone wake me, or even better... "Take Me"!
Was there not enough room on the train for me to climb aboard
The agony one feels seeing demise in a loved one's eyes
Derives a haunting verdict, on all accords
I'm left powerless, useless-No odes, codes, serum or pill
To bring you back, to make time stand still
You're vanishing, drifting ur to purgatory's align
Surrendering mercilessly to become a spectra light now frozen in time

Don't tell me you're in a better place
When I'm still here suffering, struggling with the loss & grief
Stranded, trying to understand God's plan
Do you see all of the misery trapped inside of me
Do you hear every single tear I cry
Can you feel the qualm in my missing
I'm imprisoned in my guilt
So don't tell me to go on living, when I'm barely exiting

Lashings of insanity
I sigh, I ache, and at times I feel I could break
Because no whether the tragecy
Life had no right taking you away from me
So much to say, so many promises undone-unresolved-unmade
I know I must let you go, to set you free
But how will I make it through, living on without you
There's a hole inside of me, I fill with chardonnay wine and your legacy
The party resumes, so a toast, to you my friend
True, there will be times I will hurt, grieve, agonize
But no goodbyes', fore I'll see you again

Prayers for the dying, I promise to try
Spirits having flown & still flying
May they forever outrun the sky!!!
"I Love You"! :-)

cinderfella (3rd son)

A funny thing about tyranny
And the abuse it thorns, should a mother's authority ever be scorned
Can at some point destroy the man lost inside the boy
Our calamity is Siamese & purely evident
I wish you were dead, & you never wanted me born

An agonizing truth about misery
It's resound reveres, bounded by hate, barricaded in fear
Why it impales all traces of joy & esteem
The practicality of it discerns, as I've now come to terms
You're abhorred with me, as awful as it seems

Cinderfella, The 3rd Son
Inadequate, and then some
Mama's gun, wages sum
Bury me beneath the sun

A child's dehumanizing fundamental
Its cruelty so debilitating, heinous & excruciating
Yet you spare no expense when unleashing such atrocity
Ominously, your contempt when chastising me, beats me lifelessly
The maliciousness of it exalts, as I again default
Psychological dysfunction
I, the result of sibling rivalry
Don't mean to come off crass & condescending
But what the hell makes sons #2 & #4 any better than me
I'm not ambivalent, but see what being jaded can do
They, your pearl-I, spit under your left shoe... "Well Fuck Them & You"!

Cinderfella, The 3rd Son
Fragile, yet rigid as they come
Morbidly succumbed
Not much good for anyone

You attack-For me being weak & too afraid to fight back
You disown-Take my paychecks then kick me out of your home
You curse, you belittle, ridicule, & even threaten
You are evil, you are Armageddon

The bruises, The shame, The neglect, The abuse & utter disrespect
Such legacy lounged in one's name
Oh, and I'm not even gonna mince my resentment, nor mind my breath
For holding you partially responsible for son #1's death

Where's the mother's love I'm due
Where's the acceptance & approval
I've devoted my life trying to receive from you
Why when I say "I Love You Mother"...
You reciprocate with handfuls of hate
Bragging that sons #2 & #4 are the reason why you're blessed to be alive
I may forgive, but don't expect me to ever forget-Don't hate, I'm simply
A product of what you now deplore, end result..."I declare War"!!!

Look at me now mama, (try as you might)
You can't hurt me now, You're old, I'm cold
Can you see me mama, (try as you might)
I, your disappointment, disgrace, little faggot, he's still standing
Your black sheep amounting next to nothing
Finally believing if nothing less, he's worth at least something
The boy is now lost inside this man
And I'm no longer shackled to the many lies & abuse you inflicted
over many, many, many, many, many, many, many, many years ago
I'd rather die, before I cry one damn tear so you can smile
I'd rather die, before I give you even one grandchild
Your truth is all whom now consoles, staging our reversal of roles
As the hunter now becomes the hunted
I, the 3rd son you never loved & never wanted!

n____hwhyte

Nigghahwhyte...
Where are u going tonight
And will your shame chaperone

Niggawhyte...
Preferential plight
For tonight, it's another slave master who picks over your bones

Niggahwyte...
Delusional parasite
Misconstruing self-validation for self-degradation's sin

Niggahwyte...
Manufactured appetite
To bleach the lineage out your skin, by cutting a cleft in your chin

To once again...
Simmer within social trends, those that indoctrinate ancestry's amnesty
Prejudicial overkill, a luxurious thrill for the latest House-nigga to fill
Well tell me, Mr. Shill...
How you really gon win
When you're running scared from who you are within?

Fear feeds on paranoiac truths
You crunch its brunch deliciously down
I see your face, yet in a frantic pace
You dodge mine
Buried so deep in sea of snow
Yet when the sun melts away their glow, & their hatred of race over
throes
The instant your shade everglades
Where then will you go.. "Niggahwhyte"!

whyten_____h

Whyteniggah...
Off again to the petting zoo
In search for a monkey to pleasure you

Whyteniggah...
Enticed by a line or two
Fantasizing bout what this Mandingo can do
Whyteniggah...
Prejudicial circumspect
Yet curiosity keeps your dick wet & erect

Whyteniggah...
F aux pas passion fatale
As I'm spitting & fisting up your cum-dump canal

After which, deposit me secretly back in your closet
Buried deep between boroughs a separatist's supremacy swallows
Only to be dug up, when you need to be sucked-up, plugged-up
Though fraught with the fear of being robbed & fucked-up
Negro phobia paranoia
Lest you forget the aftershocks our cultural block
That will inevitably follow

Down for the struggle, up for the cause, "Pause"...
You, coming off all loving & wholesome
While sporting tanned-face, white lips
A modern replica of that racist Son-of-a-bitch, Jolson
Trying desperately to replicate, all amenities my identity correlates
Go figure,
Cause the instant you crime-you chime...
"It wasn't me, it was the nigger"!

And to add more salt in the wound, more P.R. for the drama
I'm good enough to fuck, but to wear your name... "I'm S.O.L."!
So to hell with fuckery & congloma, you'll never see me as your equal
I'll never meet your mama

Hypocrisy's outcry,
Convinced my color is a social infectious rash
You blame my race, for your saving grace
To justify history's lie
Never will you ever see my beauty of worth & respectability
Just an indefinite improbability
Cause if I'm from an interracial blend
Hung, cut, buffed or simply dark to light-skinned
Then halleluiah, sound the trumpets ... "I'm All In"!

drug

Hey, guess what?
I tried a new drug today, It made my...

Nose bleed, heart speed
Present state hyperventilate, hallucinate
Pubes perspire, Inhibitions retire
Mouth dry, tears cry
Veins inflame
Nerves numb
Hands swell, skin pale
Delirium panic
Anguish vomit
Body shake, gut regurgitate
Ass constipate
Feet gout, my consciousness pass out
Head migraine
Strength struggle, eyes see double
Fears puff
And if all this shit wasn't enough...

I even lost my erection
Never had I imagined love's injection would wound me, incurably
Conflicted & candid-Mr. Kansas bandit, I can't let go,
I can't kick the habit
Fore everything about you, after the first fuck &..."I LOVE YOU"!
I Gotta have it, gotta have it-And God-Damn it..."I CAN'T STAND IT"!

On the level...My heart's in withdrawal mode
I feel like a zombie, a copacetic exposure-Since we departed
I've adopted time, watch ID's "True Crime",
doubled up on Chardonnay wine, while losing my mind & composure

I'm addicted, stuck inside a transl-antic state
Incoherent to sensibility, for ignorance is not bliss
Casanova Red
The venom has bled, rejection's curse, yet I choose to play dead
I shiver, I shake, religiously drape my window sills
To pill the void of now living alone sheltered in its darkness
Prognosis: Paranoiac humiliation
To escape such lease, Jesus, please give this "Love Junkie" peace
Though I've lost all acts of decency to self-idealization-Never to cease

I just wanna be free, I'll even rehab til recovery
Don't you get it, don't you see-This want for you refuses to let me be
I'm not so orthodox, nor enigmatic
Skin's pale, sanity's imbalanced, yet I can overcome such challenge
No whether our passion's limp
If you would simply forget him and return to me-to love-to we
I swear, with just a fix of your cherry-toned lips
I can again clasp my cross, toss aside misery's effigy, disavow surrender
Before this breath I breathe is snatched away
For the pastor to decree my eulogy
A mere second to detox all the hurt & hate
In order to relinquish such fate
I never wanted a fatal kiss...I only wanted closure"!

medicine

Tell me...
Why is everyone so worried about my liver
And how I'm treating em
When I die, do you plan on donating them to science
Or just plain eating em

Never you whether should I keep them simmered, stewed or pickled
In Whiskey, Vodka, Gin or Chardonnay wine
Never you mind the condition, they're doing just fine
Just dandy-In fact, hand me over that Brandy
This is my act of contrition ("Gulp")

As my brother once told me...
Mind your own, & you'll live longer
But it's apparent on this little land we call earth
Certain people make it their sole conquest to try & humidify your birth

Humor me...
Why is everybody so concerned
With how many drinks I consume
Their surveillance is a fucking nuisance, leaving microscopic traces
On a daily, weekly, monthly & yearly basis
Muthfuckas calculating, tabulating, keeping score
Even taking bets, to see if I reach a personal best
Before I fall to the floor

Did I ask for a lecture
Are you on somebody's medical board, on a "Save-a-Soul" accord
Did I request pamphlets on the many health risks drinking can cause
Pause...
Just leave me with the emotional fixture, fermenting in my elixir
And should the lord call me home-Shit, let me go
Like everyone else, I too have a right to my convictions
I bear no addition to crime, no obstruction to thoroughfare

Hell, I'm a happy drunk
Shit, it's gotta be 5pm somewhere
So to hell with all your rules & rites
Just bury me with my pride & 5th of Tequila at my side
Love, don't hate, just celebrate & stay up on out my face
Screw you & your "Love Yourself" speech
Your Damn "Amazing Grace"!

(I've got pink elephants prancing round my brain
Forgive them officer
I've try to contain them, but how can you blame them
When hypocrisy's vain has yet to abstain)

Why is that everyone who drink & drug
Psychologists, psychoanalysis, shit even pro-evangelists summarize us as
Desperate disassociates who are devoid of any kind of self-worth,
Self-love
We're just self-destructive degenerate's society crusts
And many of them either wanna commit us or just plain fuck us
Don't believe me, just hoe the streets, work the pole,
Read the paper, go to church, or ... "JUST TURN ON YOUR TV"!
Huh, you think that's insane...
I know some people that snort cocaine, while sipping on cheap
champagne
Some are back-seat freaks, dangling their feet over the front seat
Some get their fill off methamphetamine & anti-depressant pills
Others binge off food buffets, soap opera shows, latte skim & the gym
Some get their sadistic fix, off golden showers while eating shit
Some choose to elevate their mind off PCP, LSD, Child pornography, Cross
dressing or simply expressing social-Political democracy
Through ganja pipes & their artistry

So as you can see, everybody's got a vice
Mine's just happens to be in a cocktail glass
Accompanied with two cubes of ice

Understand me
This drunk fag, doesn't need a Mother's love, AA or rehab
I might be a dysfunctional punk
But fuck what ya hurrd & and don't get it twisted
I'm still a functional drunk
Not to be played nor fucked with
My face is still in the race, cause my curves still swerve
So no whether if I'm bombed, boozed, tanked or blitzed
If a slur occurs, and I'm half-way out of my wits
Word to the wise, no disrespect but...Back up off me & stay out my shit!

Some call it the Devil's poison
I say, medicine
It's my conviction, my addiction, my prescription
My liquid dependency...Care to join me?????

hoebath

Scenario 1... Kevin Stephens
Mr. Horny Heathen
I should've known from where you wanted to meet
The Heartbreak Hotel-Room # "Hump Me, Dump Me" suite
No need for febreeze or an incense, to dense or mince the sex stench
Just a quick quickie-And afterwards, not a "Thank You" nor even a hickie

Emotional emasculation
You didn't even offer me a towel after breaking my bowel
Nor engage me in casual conversation, just one "HOT" masturbation
So Dutch with your kiss and touch-You couldn't even spring for drinks
Still no time to blame, shame nor think
Just gush, then rush to the bathroom sink
To quickly do a "Poor Whore's" shower, dab on some baby powder
Cause you'll be at my house in less than an hour

Hoebath, don't laugh
At some point in life we'll all have to walk a Prostitute's path
The moment you fall in love with who doesn't know the meaning of
His eyes are quite the looker-One glance then you're swept up
(& not by chance) in his 2nd hand romance
Because everyone knows you can't transform a husband from a hooker
Boys, ya'll know the kind
He spits his shit, you take a hit, growing addicted by the minute
Then the instant his hung gets you sprung
He leaves you begging for it
Horny aftershocks, Screw a glock,
You'd better make sure your soap's stocked

Scenario 2... Mark Du Munt
You Perverted little runt
Your profile describes you as a Hillbilly hunk, greasy & sleazy
From the twang in your slang, the 8-track bangin in your 67 Mustang
Filthy beast, a real sadist's dream

Mainly because you prefer me repulsively obscene
(not to mention) partially clean
And I burn
For I'm allergic to such dehumanizing terms & bodily germs
You say "Trust", cause a little must ain't never killed anyone
And with this I spread my mouth, sop & slurp down south
And I must admit though,
Getting fucked on the hood of your truck was hot
Still, such crime shouldn't compliment the plot
So with all due respect to flesh for fantasy
Just as soon you pull out of me- This shit is going to stop

Hoebath, (Don't laugh) Just do your math
His scent should be evident-One whiff of the foul, you're screwed-Spent
As nothing can save you now
Promises of matrimony..."Don't fall for it honey"!
His definition of fidelity whom perfumes my charms
Ring the alarm,
4 minutes to strip off morality's persona & pride
To lather the loneliness you're feeling inside
Just please make certain to use a Brillo pad when scrubbing your ass
It's only obvious he's no stranger to the drips, claps & crabs
(Didn't I say don't laugh)
Girls, ya'll know the type
Floss the swipe, but can't live up to its hype

Scenario 3... Ms. Sonya Starrr (Hardee, Haar, Har,)
More appropriately, Ms. Aphrodite in a leather nightie
She seduces her Johns til they become Mr. "Love-Slaves"
Down on your knees "You know how to behave"!
Her Piranha pussy is venomous, the Black widow they say
Using everything from leather whips to prosthetic dicks
& whatever necessary elements for this Demented Dominatrix
To gain total submission of their souls and wallets
Now who'd ever suspect this coupon clippin soccer mom
A Preacher's wife, would trife to harbor such an insidious life

Though it seems Lil Ms. Bettie Page, on her last Tasmanian rage
While in the mist of having a ball with Mr. Smith
& her "Blow-Me-Up-Suzie-Doll"
Was found dead- Asphyxiated, with seven shots to her head
Suspect: Husband-Motive: Money-Defense: Alienation of affection
Anything to ensure that her life insurance policies would guarantee him a
more respectable & comfortable life

Hoebath, this cruel cool thus thou hath
Drugs, sex, rock & roll
Voulez-vous coucher avec moi, ce soir?
The underbelly of indecency beyond one's control
Soiled tampons & condoms-Hemorrhoid warts-Caligula's Sodom
This is no act for the seedy underground side of burlesque
Insensitive is the only word to describe what is grotesque
Risqué' residue, she never wanted you, at best-Odious
Missionary skank
Blood, sweat & tears smeared along seminal stained sheets
"WHEW, did you wash your ass & feet"?
Cause damn, something stinks
Funky junkie vs. Mr. Jezebel, torn panties & chipped finger nails
There never seems to be enough time to bathe,
Or get me outta this hellish maze

Look I'm sorry, but my momma didn't raise me this way
There's a rose underneath these clothes,
I take pride in my skin, even in the act of sin
But here you are hittin me up to say you're lonely again
Horny again, wantin the skinz again
My place around ten... "Oh shit, here we go again"!

friendzzzz

Hiya, I'd like to talk to you about my friendzzzz
They're...

Sweet
Warm
Kind
Caring
Loving
Gentle
Beautiful
Funny
Silly
Artistic
Prosperous
Generous
Humble
Salt of the Earth
Selfish
Lying
Trifling
Cunning, Conniving
Two-faced & Patronizing
Superficial
Back-stabbing
Users
Outright Fucking Losers
Selfish
Manipulative
Malicious
Self-righteous
Vile & Vicious
Shady
Catty
Certifiable

Cruddy & Slutty
Sick in the head
Contemptuous
Venomous
Slanderous
Subhumans
Jaded
Busted
Can't be trusted
Unpredictable, & just downright fucking despicable...Huh!

Now, tell me about your friends...

i can't fuck witchu

I can't fuck witchu
Cause the instant I see you sign online
I get giddy, giggly and gush
I become a catholic virgin
With a school-girl crush

I can't fuck witchu
Cause every single time, thoughts of you seduce my mind
I find my thighs get moist
My gut flutters, I stutter, lose consciousness
Can't catch my breath-I lose my voice
One look, & I'm butter-Once you wrap your...
Arms
Abs
Legs
Toes
Chest
Moans
Breath
Quest
Pubes
Hands
Eyes
Feet
Heat
Masculinity
Throb
Hunger
Intrigue
Snores
Pores
Around my soul
I get toxic, I can't stop it-I lose all rites & privileges to self-control
Praying to every God above you'll never let me go

True,
Stipulations were made, but they all seem to dissipate
The second we hit the sheets, & our "Bouginas" meet
Chills burn through my veins
We kiss, passive yet rough
We spoon, & instantly I fall in love
Passion vs. Promiscuity
This has got to stop
It's not healthy for either of us
Vigorously, I try to restrain
You score another whore
He referees your pain, yet I'm losing at this game

Forbidden affair, this shit is crucial
I ain't trying to get engaged
You're a loner, and I'm dysfunctional on either page
This shit is scary
Me cruising you in GBC & A4A's room
When knowing your ex is tick-tick-boom
Still, I'm consumed-Trying to prioritize my desires
Separate the fears from the fire
On the contrary, the moment our hump session starts
I begin assessing the damage
Both our baggage is doing to my heart

Friends with benefits, hoes minus pride
Black boy vs. White Boy
Both slaves to mechanical emotion
In too deep, or simply out of my head
I'm rushing home, milking my bone
Wishing I could ride yours instead

An overblown hype
I'm stressing, and you're not even my type
A thrill boulders me
I pupil your fill
And you're not even that older than me
But I see god in you
You make me wanna get accosted, fuck you til my dick gets exhausted
Flick the bitch off my shoulder
Seek religion, enlist passion's provision
Even denounce penicillin
Go stone cold sober, eternally
Til all you eat-think-drink-shit-piss-crave-rave is me
But you manipulate every angle whom dangles lies to perpetrate
Crawling to every piece of black dick
While forcing your interest in me to remain silent
Then dismiss me like I'm some fucking work client

I can't fuck witchu
I'm getting feverish every time you text
I was never clever, nor shotgun to the wise
But I'm going through extremes to cream all over your sex
John, stop looking into my eyes, it's not as if you're really liking me
You're playing a deadly hand
Round for round, each liaison is more than I can stand
(You play too fucking much)
John, you'd better stop dyking with me
You've already got me hypnotic
You're gonna fuck around and 'ma turn psychotic
Lose weight for you to carry me-Then ask you to marry me!

mr. ms. tress

Come on in
Come closer, that's it, walk straight into my sin
Let me give you the thrill of your life
One that could never be matched nor attached to your wife
Kick off your shoes, as I loosen up your tie
Are you hungry, I've prepared your favorite meal
You're home baby, so just kick back & relax
Let me cater to your every want, need, fantasy & appeal
Fore tonight, my mission is to make you feel unreal

Follow me down baby...
Let me fix you a drink while you soak in the waters of desire
Let me relieve your tension, massage your mind
Work my hands all over your body, taking you higher & higher
Watch, as I stroke your soul, from feet to hair follicle
Seduce the stress they produce, making every muscle grind
Cause I so get off watching you lose control

Let me give you more than you can stand
No judgments, no static, no masquerades, no masculine insecurities
Just one on one, you & me, man on man... "Shit, G'damn"!
Chest on chest
Flex on flex
Cock on cock
Baby, you're so fucking hot
Whispers to moans
Grind to a thrust
Sex vs. sweat... "Baby, don't cum yet"!
Hung sprung
Tongue to tongue
Kiss to kiss... "Mr. friend with Benefits"!
Sneak to freak, eruption's consumption
Come love me down, I feel your heat, I'm ready to drown

True, she lays in your bed, but I own the sheets
True, she gives you good love beyond compare
But obviously not enough to keep you there
No need for shame, suspicion or circumspect
No expectations or idle threats
No disrespect...
But fuck your bitch & brats
That your obligation
It's not where I'm living at
Amicable arrangement, I play my part on the sidelines
So to hell with false modesty, D.L's impropriety, morale's wavering pride
Respectfully...I'm your mr. ms. tress
Your dick on the side!!!

the tears of st. john

I should've resisted your charms
But I was enchanted the instant you smiled
So dashingly debonair, I must be walking on air
Slowly melting away
Like an Ivory candle, as I touched your shadow
Each time you turned away

Alexey's Russian ball, the unveiling of reverie's splendor
Like an opus serenading the heavens
One touch, and I was swept beyond surrender
Intoxicated, as you stared deep into my eyes
Soothing my heart's cavity
Feeling him rhapsodize

I dreamt of Sunsets in Budapest, sipping tea in Tuscany
Walking along cobble-stoned streets beneath London's fog
After making love beneath Charles' bridge in Prague

Still, just as with any dream, it ends
To acquaint with an agonizing truth one must contend...
For the tears of St. Jean
Knew that daring arms where passion resides
Would tranquilize my soul
Enchain me to your lies

Seduced & bewitched
Seconds before the waltz, moments after we kissed
The overture underscores, as a hush turns to a roar
Fydor Chaliapin takes to the stage
I reach my hand over to the next chair & find you're no longer there
Next page...

His Imperial Supreme
The beauty you flaunt-So Adonis, so gallant
Unleashing confectionery appeal
Its carousel canopies
Stealing my breath, bending my will
Oh why tonight, did the stars spill a silver lining's chill

Illuminated ambiance silken round passion's embroidery
Stealing mystical pleasures and their forbidden treasures
We worship, we encrust
Tasting Tunisian champagne the rains shower upon us
A simple theatrical gesture, you play the part brilliantly
Inseparably, why has thou bequeath me

I dreamt of Chateau's & Cathedrals in Vienna,
Holding hands in Amsterdam
Swimming nude along the banks of the Mediterranean Sea
Right after dining alongside of aristocracy at Hofburg's diamond Jubilee

Yet, like with all fairy tales, a monster lurks
There to snatch your breath, flight you unto the river of death...
For the dance of Balanchine
Would for sure, captivate me to your allure
With every step, our passion was magnanimously kismet
Only for you to now act as if we've never met

In with laughter, out with the crowd
The carnival was lovely...But where are you now?

A Harlequin hallmark
How was I to know or even conceive
Such an affair, was a journey to the land of nowhere
Love's myth, a correlated bliss
Its novella billows, sinking my surrealistic pillow
Though daunted, I reminisce its renaissance

Feeling the stinging of strings, the haunting of a flute & harp
Tears segue way a phantom's masquerade
To foyer the breaking of one's heart

Alas,
Sweet slumber
A spell once chosen, now undoubtedly has been broken
Fore the peasant, left to the whims of a romance unfounded
Finds his prince has fictitiously absconded
Photographic apparitions regaled, orchestrating soliloquy's hell
Now aligns paltry memories locked away somewhere in time
Pages bleed, as they tear off into the sea
Epilogue, a love remembered
Is now all that is left for me...And the tears of St. Jean!!!

(Come back into these arms again, My darling
Oh how they hunger for your embrace
Kiss me & caress me-Make love to me as you did once
Oh my darling, come back to me again"!)

night of porn

Tonight,
I want no romantic dinners
No flowers, candy or expensive gifts
Tonight,
I wanna be a sinner
Relinquish all power, for my love to come down & my legs to lift

Tonight,
I wanna strip out my inhibitions to soak in your sweat
Lose my virginity, like I did back in 1983
Tonight,
My plight bares no convictions, he's maximized
A welcomed conversion into sexual perversion
One who embodies queer chastity
Merely to implore the filth of your every fantasy

Tonight, make me a night of porn
Make me make you go all the way
Risqué roleplay
My body is tight, taut, & pornographically hot
Simply for your viewing & doing pleasure
For I swear every time we're together, I become one slut-stock
Let's get crazy-wild
PNP hungrily, then fuck each other non-stop

Tonight
Treat me like sop a pig slops
Wear the look of lust when thrusting your tongue in my mouth
Tonight, when you bite, make me struggle & fight
Mush in my must, slide inside my backside
Crud the mud, stem my rosebud

Tonight
Let's feed our flesh an orgy of masochistic debauchery
Grind my mind, spoon my womb erect & wet, but don't cum just yet
Tonight, make my soul squirm with delight, lose control
This is a matter of life & death
I'm not looking 4 just mouth 2 mouth
But for you to make me lose my breath

Make my body a night of Porn
Dominate, Hogtie-No questions... No Lies
The idle mind is a playground for the devil
I know this boy's cunt is what you want
Still no flames to tame, if you can't go for broke when choking my throat
While I'm calling out your name
Make me weak, Fuck me rough & raw
Til where I can hardly speak, barely crawl
Make me a night of porn
Make it sleazy for you & I
The name of the game-The electrifying pleasure to pain
See it as an anniversary present, so no rules apply

Let's bathe in a twisted Sodom, (with or without a condom)
Let's make tonight unlike no other...Unforgettable
By sexing so sadistic, so deviant, so...Unrespectable

BDSM Kissing
Glory holes & fisting
Golden showers, hour after hour
Spank me with the wood
Harder, and I'll be good
Cop my g-spot
Make me suck sins & secrets out your cock
Use, abuse my cumdump
Make it jump, jilt & split
Can't wet it, spit on that shit
Faster & faster, fuck me harder you bastard
Toes curl, rhythmic twitch

Oh here it comes, what's my name...
Shadow
Sinz
Diaz
Allen
Austin
Rollins
Wolfe
Von Fistenburg
Neal
Riley
Wyler
Peters
Douglas
Hunt
Hughes
Romero
Parker
Flynn
Lamaar
Hurston
Long
Sly & Fyerfli
Donovan
York
Fisk
and of course, "Davis"...("Strang Bitch, that is, lol"!)

american life/american dream enter view (pt.1)

So...
How did you achieve the American Dream?
Well let's see, I...

Milked

Bilked

Stole

Hoed

Lied

Connived

Licked

Sucked

Fucked

Kissed

Pissed

Shitted

Cheated

Savagely defeated

Everyone I ever knew

With no "May I, PLEASE or even a GOD-DAMNED THANK YOU"!

☺

caveman (pt.2)

Tell me again, why am I bitch
Is it that I'm too bitter
Or is it that good men are hard to find
I've been scolded for being too choosy, cynical, eccentric, emotional
& on occasions even anal & analytical
But is it really a crime to not sell-out
Yet to hold-out for what's rightfully mine

Hell on earth, I rise from my bed
Shake another hangover out of my head
Tug on my girth
Wearily checking into my mirror-& although I'm fierce as fuck
I fit, because I'm still shit out of luck
I've traveled many places, slept with many cultures, continents
& their races
But I'm starting to believe he'll never appear, he'll never bliss
Hopelessly desire less, cause for me he just doesn't exist
So I'm left just...

Searching for my caveman
My Love Supreme-My Fuck De uxe
The one to rescue my lair-By kissing my heart while pulling my hair
I'm looking for that ultimate playmate
My warrior, my eternal soul mate
My passion's jubilee, tell me... "ARE YOU HE"?

Tell me true, why am I still single
Has my glitter lost its gold, or have I simply gotten too fat, too old
Locked inside a frustrating circumstance, I must be penis poison
Cause when other men are around me,
they get allergic to wedding bands

Tears that Jesus' wept, I'm swept up in the need to please my king
So I oblige his every pleasure whom measures meth, coke, PNP
A night of drunken sex, shadowboxing taken out of context
And just before I climax, he runs out on me

Heart's imprisonment
Disillusioned, discontentment
It seems as if I'm forever saying hello to goodbye
Emotionally emasculated, I expose
My logic bends, in & out of gay trends
Still I must contend
With the truth that this whirlwind may never end
No need for rehearsing,
Especially when it's my heart that's constantly thirsting...

For my caveman
My phantom, my love's fantasy
The Zephyr to my Zen-My aromatherapy every now & then
The reason why god made men for men
Like back in the day when love between the 2 was organic,
was old-school
Unconditional surrender, I'd sacrifice my all
To savor in every flavor his essence transcends

Fraudulent epidemic
Why are the men I tend to meet
Are not only frugal, fickle, despicably egotistical
And only seem to be into the Gym, Latte and oh by the way...
My caramel pickle
Must I compromise my fate, my dreams, my worth & weight
In order for you to see me beyond the sheets
In order for my circle of one to be complete
If not today, will tomorrow be too late

Don't get me wrong
I don't need you smothering me like a London's fog
Or all over me like Georgia muc on a Texas hog
A man of worth totally homegrown
No need for outside validation, I stand firm on my own
Somebody, please rescue me from the plight my fight keeps cursing
incessantly thirsting...

For my caveman
Mi papi- my captor
The one who seduces my dreams, then makes love to me right after
Screw conviction, my intuition surmises
Look into my eyes, I know he exists
So he must be alive
The one to release every chair ingrained around my heart's tower
His power, his truth, his passion, fears, flaws, love, valor, voice, eyes &
every tear they cry
Make or break, he is the promise my soul stakes
Mi Amore...Need I say anymore?

church home

The shades are drawn, the lights are drowned
All the money is spent, music & phones are shut off
People are gone... "It's now just you & me"...

Sober & naked on bended knees
Hopeless & helpless, though surrendering all
Alone in your presence, I feel a sense of calm
As I pray for your mercy & grace
To save me from all improbabilities toiled in life's atrocities
To free me of my sins, to strengthen my faith

You've given me a love I've never known
You've been a true confidant in times of trouble & strife
Lord you are everything to me, for I am nothing without you
I surrender to you my life
You're a savior...
When family & friends forsake me
When the world constantly tries to break me
You lift my soul, steady its sail
Wash away my pain, pour peace into my hell

I'm not ashamed to cry, I'm not afraid to testify
No judgments or fears, because you said come as you are
So here I stand, in all that I was & am
Praising & claiming your holy name
Thanking you for saving this troubled man
Even in times of anger, frustration & doubt, locked in my sorrows
Seeing no way out
In my heart I guess I've always known
That no matter where I've been or may go
I can always run to you
Even in times when I stumble, I shall remain serviced, humbled

Blood & bone, forever hastened to your throne
You are my light, my rock, the center of my joy
My church home, which is why I never walk alone
My spiritual source on all accords
I love you, and I say... "Yes Lord"!

i cannot grow with nepotism

boyz burlesque

As a little boy, I always dreamed of being a star, someone special
And by far, no matter how awkward & I ugly I was
Or all the times I was never told how much I am loved
I always believed that somebody would 1 day come & rescue me... "From Me"!

As man I've always desired for someone to believe in me
To fill my soul with acknowledgments & accolades
Make me feel wanted, needed & beautiful
Oh, the price my pride has paid
Believing my life would then be saved, watching my heart seduce,
yet deduce any specs of self-preservation & self-respect
Never once realizing that self-love isn't a hand-out, it's not a prospect
And the only way you'll ever stand-out, is by forgiving your own sins
& loving you from within

And so I dance...
For a mother who at times is so loving & yet so foreign to me
For the many friends who have died at my side
For the many suitors I've sexed, yet always left wondering...
"What's Next"?
For the many sleepless nights on other people's floors & sofa beds
For the many eat less nights I silently cried & prayed
While roaches & rats crawled above my head
For the men on death row
& those in the state or fed pen doing life or ten
For the seniors living in a cardboard cage, existing on a SSI wage
For the mothers raising their kids with only beans & wieners in the fridge
(a stale loaf of bread & a bottle of sprite with no fizz)
For the many living with aids, alcohol & substance dependencies
For a cure that will one day heal the world of all its ill-willed ignorance,
senseless wars & their catastrophic atrocities
For every child being bullied, beaten, killed or raped
For "If I should die before I wake, I pray to you Lord my soul to take"!

For politicians & priests to one day fight together for freedom & peace
For the many like me,
In the hopes that such a dance will irreversibly cease

I dance drunkenly-Incoherently searching for worth & esteem
Lost in a dream whom wades inside me...Soberly
I dance through misery, misconceptions, indiscretions condoned
I dance, for the Lord says that shall I walk with him, I'll never walk alone
I dance no matter the loneliness, emptiness or how much I am penniless
Nonetheless, I dance,
Because today I dare to saturate my soul in happiness
I dance
No matter even with all the Grey in my hair, gout in my feet
I still keep up, I don't miss a beat
I dance even when my strength can't go on,
I dance for the spirits that keeps me, they say to me...
Anari, your work is far from done...
"So dance on, dance on"!
I dance, I dance more than this ole life of mine can stand, I dance,

Fore...
No whether how technical, limbo, partnered or solo
No whether if the notes & key to the song is all wrong
I too have a place in this world, fore I too belong
Through laughter, tears, through hysterics or dreams
No whether beguiled or bullied
I am the dream-maker, his artful dodger, sojourn's light
No matter all the evil this life has yet to digress, I'm never distressed
You will find me dancing day or night
Solely believing one day the boy lost inside this man
Will one day be given his chance, to see a brighter tomorrow
& to dance!!!!

no, your girl can't watch

I knew it, from the day we first met at church
I had to have you between my thighs
And I knew you wanted inside
The way you flirted back was only obvious
The lust lurking from within your eyes, you was ready to attack
Our vibe was intense, our attraction was forbidden & palpable
I wanted to get nasty & naughty, wrap all my love around your body
Right there in the parking lot
And when you approached to broach a date
My senses trembled, my body went hot, but wait...

One wrench I didn't see coming, when you proposed a Menage-a-Trois
Destroyed any chance for a one night stand
Especially finding out that it wouldn't be with another man
Yet your other life that belongs to her... "Your wife"!
Shocked & dismayed, yet all I can say is...

No, your girl can't watch
I don't give a fuck, if she's the ride picking you up
No, your girl can't watch
I don't give a damn if she is hot to trot
If you think mama's gonna be the one calling the shots
On how daddy plays in this baby's twot... "NOT"!

Eyes lead blind sometimes
I was thrown to utter devastation, fore I wasn't aware of your reputation
Though being such a gorgeous guy, I could see why so many stand in line
Because you are fine as all out doors
And I'm dying to have your cum clog my pores
But no matter how sticky & wet, my fantasies may get
Such twisted proclivities will never seduce my curiosity
No ever get the best of me

Because the only voyeur that better be lurking in my foyer
Is a man-In every aspect, concept of a masculine define
If he expects even a percentage of this ass of mine

No, your girl can't watch
No disrespect, but I'm not into that kind of sex
As we going the rounds,
I'm disrupted from the sounds of her gyrating her hips,
Licking her lips, tugging on her tits
Sliding her hand down south to finger-fuck her cli_t

Shit, all I can say is "Fuck"
The baritone in your breath is mesmerizing, your body is taut & tight
With a monster dick that's thick & ripe, and with the kind of sex I like
We would've tore some shit up, to where we both begged to get up
Still, nothing doing-So don't try plying me with weed, Courvoisier & meth.

Wild sex, while high off X, thinking I'll trust a try... "Oh no, not I"!
You see I can't fake the funk, cunt is not what I want
So she can't regulate nor participate
I'm not giving her any dick dildo or shower nozzle masturbation material
To take home for you two to enjoy, on youtube or your flat screen TV
To quench a thirst so perverse, damn horny freaks

While I'm being groped & caressed
There she is cooped up in the corner watching us get undressed
My declaration is not up for negotiation nor debate
Save your static, she can't even see us suck-face, tea-bag or masturbate
You've got the wrong boy
But if that's what it's to be
In order for you & me to explore queer carnality
Then may I suggest... "You Kindly Cut The Concrete"!
And be sure to take yo bitch witcha
No love-loss here, I damn sho won't miss ya!

About The Author

Anari "Strang" Davis personifies what it means to be "Organic" when it comes to his artistry. "I've always had a bizarre visceral when expressing myself"! To never stand on ceremony but to always achieve the highest of plateaus, for it is what I believe to be the true testimony of one's art.

A producer, writer & activist, Anari has never been one to divulge into just one dynamic especially when it comes to his LGBT community. I feel as though I have a direct responsibility to not only through my art but my entire being to never just be another "Gay Man"! I wanted to have a voice.

Which would come through several projects such ranging from his activism, a benefit he produced in 2011 titled..."ALL THAT DRAG"! A variety show designed to entertain audiences while in the same vein raising proceeds to be donated to variable charities those that continue their advocacy & in the fight against HIV/AIDS! A fixture within the artist's underground communities, he's done everything from spoken word, directed fashion & high end art shows penned several books which includes the heavily anticipated upcoming release..."BOYZ BURLESQUE"! "A theatrical humanization told through the eyes of man"! (he describes it)

Boyz Burlesque was truly a spiritual awakening for me, a cathartic trance. I felt it was extremely necessary to tear to shreds off society's contradictions & superficial standards that so many of us men fall prey to. But without preaching a standardized dynamic. Life's examples ranging from child abuse & prostitution, sexual proclivities, coping with the loss of loved ones, substance & alcohol abuse, spousal abuse & many other lil surprises. I wanted to capture the naked essence of being a man & not by one's ideal decree or protocol.

Links:

http://www.linkedin.com/pub/anari-davis/33/283/a90/
https://www.facebook.com/stranguprods
https://www.facebook.com/Bleustrang

About Glover Lane Press

Thank you so much for your purchase of this extraordinary book by Strang!

Glover Lane Press is honored to be the publishing house for passionate and thought provoking poetry!

If you enjoyed reading Boyz Burlesque, by Strang, please visit our website for our new, featured and upcoming publications.

Azaan Kamau started Glover Lane Press in the summer of 2000 to give a voice to poets, journalists, and writers worldwide. Azaan and Glover Lane Press have helped countless individuals publish and distribute media in print and in digital formats.

As a woman, one of Azaan's publishing goals is to focus on marginalized or over-looked communities of writers, poets, artist, and photographers. Azaan feels everyone has a story that must be heard or recorded. Another important goal is to use the proceeds from sales of Azaan's books to improve the lives of people around the world. Azaan's companies will feed the hungry, house the homeless, heal the sick, educate and eradicate disease, etc!

Visit us at Gloverlanepress.webs.com

Like Us on Facebook:
Facebook.com/Gloverlanepress

www.ingramcontent.com/pod-product-compliance
Lightning Source LLC
Chambersburg PA
CBHW052126090426
42741CB00009B/1969